"I have known Sandie Freed for many years. This book is about becoming a freedom fighter—freedom from Satan's lies about us. Sandie writes so well about this subject because she lives the book. She knows what it takes to be free from Satan's lies. I love Sandie and I love this book."

—**Barbara J. Yoder,** senior pastor of Shekinah Christian Church; international speaker and author; apostolic leader, Breakthrough Apostolic Ministries Network, Ann Arbor, Michigan

"When Sandie Freed says she is 'addicted to freedom' she means it! Sandie is like the coach or manager you see in the corner talking to the champ between rounds in a great boxing match. A true 'freedom fighter' herself, Sandie takes everything she paid a price to learn and deposits it with clarity and power into your hands in *Silencing the Accuser*. I only wish there were more books like this around when I began my spiritual journey. It would have made life easier. Read it and share it with others!"

—**Dr. Lance Wallnau,** president, Lance Learning Group

SILENCING

THE

ACCUSER

SILENCING

THE

ACCUSER

SANDIE FREED

Chosen
a division of Baker Publishing Group
Grand Rapids, Michigan

Published by Chosen Books
11400 Hampshire Avenue South
Bloomington, Minnesota 55438
www.chosenbooks.com

Chosen Books is a division of
Baker Publishing Group, Grand Rapids, Michigan.

Printed in the United States of America

In keeping with biblical principles of creation stewardship, Baker Publishing Group advocates the responsible use of our natural resources. As a member of the Green Press Initiative, our company uses recycled paper when possible. The text paper of this book is comprised of 30% post-consumer waste.

Library of Congress Cataloging-in-Publication Data

Freed, Sandie.
    Silencing the accuser : eight lies Satan uses against Christians / Sandie Freed ; foreword by Bill Hamon.
        p.   cm.
    Includes bibliographical references (p.   ).
    ISBN 978-0-8007-9510-8 (pbk. : alk. paper)   1. Spiritual warfare.   2. Bible. O.T. Job—Criticism, interpretation, etc.   I. Title.
    BV4509.5.F748   2011
    235'.4—dc22
                                                                    2011002692

*I dedicate this book to the original and true
Freedom Fighter, my Lord and Savior,
Jesus Christ.*

*Thank You, Lord Jesus, for Your desire to
defeat my enemies and set me free.*

*Thank You for Your precious blood that is
incorruptible, cleansing and restoring and
that delivers me from the Accuser.*

"If therefore the Son shall make you free,
ye shall be free indeed."

JOHN 8:36, ASV

CONTENTS

FOREWORD

Sandie Freed has blessed the people of God with books revealing vital truths. This book on silencing the Accuser and exposing eight lies he uses against Christians will set many free. This is a must-read for every Christian who wants to be free and victorious in his or her Christian life.

I appreciate Sandie's willingness to write liberating biblical truth that upsets the devil but blesses God's people. She writes with boldness, knowing that greater is the Christ within her than the devil and all his demons. Understanding how your enemy shoots at you creates a defensive shield of faith that can stop all his fiery darts. Knowing the tactics and strategies of the enemy is essential in gaining victory over him.

I understand the attacks the enemy tries to bring against authors of biblical truth. I have written numerous books on present truth during my 56 years of ministry. All believers, including authors and frontline ministers, need a strong intercessory group to be a shield around them, providing protection from attack.

This book will give you wisdom and insight to discern the accusations of Satan. When we know the truth, it frees us to serve God fully and be victorious Christians, able to minister freedom to others.

We should never be afraid of upsetting the devil. He hates all Christians and is dedicated to deceiving and destroying everyone who will listen to him. God promises throughout Scripture, on the other hand, that He will fight the enemy of those who proclaim His Son, Jesus, as the only way to walk, the only truth to believe and the only life to live.

God bless you, Sandie, with divine health, protection and long life to keep blessing Christ's people around the world. You are more than a conqueror and are enabling thousands to be more than conquerors through the truths presented in your books.

This book will enable many to silence the accuser and walk free of his false accusations. Read it as a warrior would read a war manual. As you practice these truths, you will be an overcomer and receive Christ's rewards to His overcomers.

DR. BILL HAMON, AUTHOR, *THE DAY OF THE SAINTS* **AND OTHERS**

BISHOP, CHRISTIAN INTERNATIONAL APOSTOLIC NETWORK (CIAN)

ACKNOWLEDGMENTS

Over the years I have received many testimonies of how my books have blessed others. Some have even said, "Sandie, your book changed my life." I am always excited and humbled to know that the revelation and insight the Lord shares with me empowers others. It is important, however, for me to thank many others who have helped make my writing possible. As some have said, "It takes a village." Well, for me to write, this is true.

I want especially to thank each of my personal intercessors for continuing to cover me in prayer as I write. Thank you for standing in the gap for me as I seek God for more revelation and attempt to pen what I receive from heaven.

A special thanks to Paula Bledsoe, who spends countless hours not only praying for me as an intercessor, but also editing my articles and manuscripts.

I want to thank my precious sister, Pam, who is still the wind beneath my wings in so many ways. Thank you for your love and support over the years and especially for your devotion to the Kingdom of God.

To my Zion family: Without you our First Friday Fire would not be able to continue. Because of your commitment to the Lord, we are still empowered to touch so many others. May the Lord bless you abundantly.

I wish to honor my spiritual parents, Bishop and Mom Evelyn Hamon. You have believed in me and have empowered me to continue to fly. Thank you for your spiritual impartation and wisdom.

I want to thank Dr. Jim Davis, who is my theological advisor for every book I write. He and his wife, Jeanni, are our special friends whom I honor with all my heart.

Once again, I want to thank two very special people who co-labor with me. To Jane Campbell, editorial director of Chosen Books, and my editor, Grace Sarber, I cannot thank you enough for your continued support through every project. I am so grateful that the Lord connected us.

And as always, I want to thank my faithful husband, who continues to stand with me and encourage me through every project. Thank you for over 37 years of marriage and a wonderful life together.

INTRODUCTION

Put on the whole armor of God, that ye may be able to stand against the wiles of the devil. For our wrestling is not against flesh and blood, but against the principalities, against the powers, against the world-rulers of this darkness, against the spiritual (hosts) of wickedness in the heavenly (places).

EPHESIANS 6:11–12, ASV

Freedom. It is worth fighting for. And its benefits are appreciated more if one has experienced an imprisonment or captivity.

A mere seven-letter word, *freedom* speaks volumes to those of us who have felt the grip of the Accuser. And we all have been targeted by the plans of the enemy. John 10:10 reminds us that we have a thief who desires to steal, kill and destroy. Satan seeks opportunities to seduce us with his lies and entice us into sin. Sin opens a wide door to our adversary and enables him to target us relentlessly. Romans points out that we have all sinned and come short of the glory of God. We all, therefore, have felt the grip of confinement as we have pursued our destiny in God.

Freedom implies being free from restraints and oppression.

The opposite of freedom is slavery. When one is a slave, he or she becomes a possession. To think that when I am held captive to Satan because of unbelief or sin—or anything else that opposes God—I become his slave. Unfortunately, many of us have become enslaved to Satan's bondage; we have become puppets as our Accuser pulls our strings. Many of us are enslaved to the bondage, or yokes, of our past. Shame, discouragement, disillusionment, despair and hopelessness are a few of the yokes with which we suffer on a daily basis. We remain helpless because we do not recognize Satan's wiles and do not know how to break free.

Beloved, this book will empower you to launch into more freedom. It will unlock many hidden mysteries concerning the ways your enemy attempts to abort your future. If you have been knocking at the door for revelation and asking God for freedom and victory, then God is answering your prayers. Jeremiah 33:3 says, "Call to Me and I will answer you and show you great and mighty things, fenced in and hidden, which you do not know (do not distinguish and recognize, have knowledge of and understand)" (AMP).

For me, freedom has become an addiction; I seek it more and more every day. I do not want anything—ungodly belief systems, religious traditions, ungodly addictions or the wiles of the devil—to hinder my transformation. I therefore consider myself a "freedom fighter." In fact, this title was given to me when I ministered to a congregation of believers in the state of Washington, and I realized it was a mantle of authority given by God. I embraced it then and I am even more committed to fighting for freedom today. But I do not simply fight for my own freedom; I press into heaven to help set *you* free.

If you have read any of my previous books, you know that my intention is to expose the many wiles of the enemy. The term *wiles* is derived from a Greek word, *methodeia,* which is where we get our English word *method.* It denotes "trickery" and gives a picture of the enemy "lying in wait" to destroy us.[1] The word speaks to the way the enemy devises schemes to attack and defeat his prey. In *Sliencing the Accuser,* your eyes will be opened to the many seductions of the Accuser—the adversary who continually seeks to deceive you. You will become increasingly aware of the Accuser's various methods to hold you captive to your past traumas, shame and addictions.

Beloved, Ephesians 6:12 speaks truth: We are not warring against flesh and blood as we obtain victory. We are warring against principalities, powers, rulers of darkness and spiritual wickedness in high places. The Accuser seeks to destroy us, so we must destroy him. The only way to break free from a yoke of slavery is to destroy the yoke.

To battle this stronghold, we must put on the entire armor of God and move forward into spiritual warfare. The helmet of salvation is one of our spiritual weapons to battle against the enemy. It covers the head and will therefore empower our minds to receive new truths and to understand fully the wiles of our enemy. Our minds must be renewed so that we can become transformed into His image. As you read this book, your mind will be challenged. Be open to receive new truths, and expect warfare in this area. To be forewarned is to be forearmed. Let us therefore arm ourselves for the battle.

Before we begin, let's pray this prayer together:

Father God, I am aware that I am about to receive fresh revelation concerning the wiles of the Accuser. I lay hands on my head and ask that You protect my mind as I read. I am ready for Your Holy Spirit to speak to me. I know that Your Word, according to Jeremiah 1:12, says that You will watch over Your Word to perform it. Thank You for protecting me from the lion that seeks to steal, kill and destroy. Father, I am knocking at the door and requesting fresh revelation that will empower me to walk in freedom I believe to receive. In Jesus' name, Amen.

Are you ready for victory? I know you are, and I am so excited that you have committed to take this journey with me. This freedom fighter wants you to be free indeed. Fighting for freedom requires commitment and determination. Keep calling out to God. Keep knocking, and He will open the doors that have blocked your freedom.

There is no great victory without a great battle. Prepare yourself for an incredible victory against your Accuser. You, too, are called to be a "freedom fighter."

THE ACCUSER

One day as the angels came to present themselves before the LORD, Satan, the Accuser, came with them.

JOB 1:6, TLB

The day had arrived when the angels were to present themselves to the Lord to give an account of their activities. Without question, each angel knew to be there and was excited to share his observations of the saints. Each one looked forward to being with the Lord and becoming more equipped to be His messenger and minister upon the earth.

"Get out of my way!" Satan pushed his way past the other angels. He smiled as he pressed through the crowd, thinking that coming to heaven's throne room was *his* idea.

Satan's presence in heaven's court caused quite a commotion. "What is *he* doing here?" the angels wondered. He had been cast out of heaven. What brought him here now? How was he allowed entrance?

"Remember," one wise angel interrupted, "Yahweh knows all things. He must have allowed this."

God sat majestically on His throne, totally unmoved by Satan's presence. He knew Satan's intentions. Indeed, Satan had entered God's court only because God Himself had allowed it. The Lord observed Satan's pride and arrogance. *He will never learn that I alone am God and what I say goes. He is my pawn yet does not realize it.* God saw the whole plan laid out before Him. He knew the evil intent in Satan's heart as the Accuser manipulatively planned to plead his case against God's son and servant, Job. God also knew that Job would prove to be righteous. God loves to prove His children faithful and then to smile at the devil when they pass his tests. God also had an ultimate plan for Job: He would allow Job to suffer to prove Job's righteousness to Satan, to Job himself and ultimately to all of creation.

"Let him come forth." The Lord's voice flowed over the court-room like liquid. All heard the voice of Living Water as it cleared and cleansed the atmosphere. Only righteous judgment would prevail, and God had set the tone.

Satan stepped forward and stood before the throne of God. Bent on destroying man, he was the adversary of all God loved. The Lord addressed him. "Where have you been?" As if He did not know.

Satan explained that he had been roaming throughout the earth, walking up and down in it. God observed Satan's pompous snicker as he bragged about his roaming. He knew that this evil creature was like a roaring lion seeking those he might devour. God's thoughts raced with His love for Job, and He smiled as He thought of His servant. *I know Job will remain sober and vigilant even when tempted,* He thought. Job would be proven and, therefore, blessed beyond measure for his patience and perseverance—traits that even Job did not know he had. God planned for Job to love Him even more after this proving process. Yet knowing Satan must give an account of his wanderings upon the earth, God pointedly addressed Satan's observations of Job.

"And have you considered My servant Job? I am quite certain that there is none like him. Job is completely blameless. He walks uprightly before Me and shuns evil. He is a man who fears Me. I can completely trust him as My loyal servant."

Satan's back heaved, and his every hair stood on end. His countenance grew even more evil, and he exposed himself as the demonically possessed creature he was, ready to pounce on his prey. "Well, sure, Job walks uprightly and remains loyal to You. You have placed a hedge of protection around him. Who wouldn't serve You if he was surrounded by wealth and blessings? In fact, You even go so far as to make others believe that You *guarantee* a life of blessings."

Satan had hoped his darkness would dilute the glory of God in the court. Yet God's Light completely snuffed it out as He remained focused on His eternal plan concerning Job.

Satan pushed for an opportunity to put Job on trial. "If You will only stretch out Your hand and strike everything He has, then You will realize he is not as righteous as You think. I tell You this: Job will curse You to Your face."

The Lord rose from His throne. His glory was so brilliant that Satan fell on his face. Darkness cannot stand in the presence of God's *shekinah* glory. Satan grew a little fearful now.

"From now on, Satan, I will consider you the Accuser—one who falsely accuses those who belong to Me. I intimately know Job, and although I am not subject to your whims, I will allow you to strike. I give you permission to take all that My servant, Job, has. I will prove to you that Job is My loyal son, and at the end of his testing he will be more blessed. You will curse the day you asked to falsely accuse My children. But you, Accuser, will not lay a finger on Job; you cannot take his life." Satisfied but with an uneasy feeling in his gut, Satan left the presence of the Lord.

Placing His scepter by His side, God sat back on His throne. His thoughts were on Job. He smiled, light beams jetting outward from His face, and His heart leapt at the thought of Job's loyalty and obedience. God knew Job and was confident that Job's awesome reverence of God continuously empowered him to hate evil—in whatever form it appeared. As the Lord thought about Job, His heart grew with love for him, and it was as if His heartbeat of love for Job became a cadence in heaven. Heaven was in unity; each angel heard the words of God's heart. Peace resounded in the court of heaven. Job would endure the fiery furnace because God had committed to be in the fire with him.

> To fear the LORD is to hate evil; I hate pride and arrogance, evil behavior and perverse speech. Counsel and sound judgment are mine; I have understanding and power. By me kings reign and rulers make laws that are just; by me princes govern, and all nobles who rule on earth. I love those who love me, and those who seek me find me. With me are riches and honor, enduring wealth and prosperity. My fruit is better than fine gold; what I yield surpasses choice silver. I walk in the way of righteousness, along the paths of justice, bestowing wealth on those who love me and making their treasuries full.
>
> PROVERBS 8:13–21

A CLOSER LOOK AT THE BOOK OF JOB

I have always had a vivid imagination. I like to imagine different Bible characters—how they dressed, what they felt, how their culture affected their religious belief systems. I imagine their dialogues, facial expressions and private conversations with God. I imagine their challenges, their mental anguish as they faced decisions and even their fear. I believe God allows spaces between the lines of His Word to challenge our imaginations and prompt our hearts to press into deeper revelation.

Yet who really wants to imagine himself in Job's situation? To be honest, none of us does. I have secretly prayed I would never have to endure such testing, and I imagine many of us have prayed such a prayer. Yet I also have opposed the same Accuser throughout my lifetime. Each of us has. The same evil Accuser who accused Job before the throne of the Most High God is the same Accuser with whom each of us contends, especially if we have a burning heart to know God intimately and to serve Him. The book of Job is noted by many to be the first book of the Bible that was put on paper. How amazing that this narrative was the one the Holy Spirit chose to be penned first! While the Bible begins with Genesis, that book actually was written years later than the book of Job.

The book's champion, Job (*Iyyob* in Hebrew), is an example of a righteous man who walked in integrity and eventually endured tremendous suffering but never blamed God. Though he had many questions and many times asked God why, Job submitted to his Lord's faithfulness. More than thirty chapters are devoted to Job's searching his soul. Attempting to find a reason for his misfortune, he debated his friends, who were influenced by the Accuser (discussed in the next chapter). Yet after the exhausting and tragic encounters, Job no longer cared why because his heart had melted into continual worship.

Job is one of the most misunderstood books of the Bible. Many theologians view the book of Job strictly from a legalistic perspective, rather than from a compassionate insight. Sometimes experiencing a crisis ourselves empowers us to view Scripture differently—in a more compassionate way that allows us to see the true heart of God written on each page. Perhaps Job journaled his thoughts, concerns, heartaches and conversations with his "comforters." Who else but Job himself could have explained his pain with so much detail? For Job to have referred to himself as "righteous" may seem somewhat pompous, but maybe he simply and truly understood his relationship with God.

Yet many theologians believe Job was not the actual author. If that is so, then why would the book's unknown author have written about the fiery tests of Job? Perhaps the Holy Spirit divinely inspired another man to write objectively but with supernatural insight into Job's righteousness and faithfulness during the testing process. Perhaps he was given insight into the heavenly courts to document the approach of Job's Accuser and then write in such a way that we all could benefit from understanding and relating to Job's fiery trials.

At the time Job was tested, no other books of the Bible had been written. He had no Word to quote, no documented previous wilderness experiences to empower him, no scriptural promises to encourage him, no Scriptures to quote to his Accuser. But what he did possess was a deep-seated, heartfelt, Holy Spirit-inspired relationship with God to hold him up during dark times.

SATAN IN GOD'S PRESENCE?

It has always puzzled me why the Lord allowed Satan into His presence in the first place. Satan had been cast out of heaven, yet he was allowed to come before God's throne along with the heavenly angels.

The enemy of our souls presumed to approach God's glory, yet there is no light in him. I imagine that the evil one's darkness would have been completely consumed by God's light and fiery presence. The light would have obliterated every inch of the devil, and there would be nothing but empty space left where Satan once stood. He would have been fried right on the spot. Or I imagine that as the River of God washed through Satan's evil being he was melted into nothingness, like the evil witch in *The Wizard of Oz* when Dorothy tossed water upon her.

I do not believe for one minute that Satan was allowed entrance unless God ordered it. All power belongs to God and to Him alone. Yet God *did* allow Satan into His presence for a reason and purpose that *God* had planned. He allowed Satan to test Job for a divine reason: to prove Job's future to Satan, and to Job himself. I believe even Job did not realize the strength of his faith until he was forced to overthrow the Accuser. Job's worshipful heart was the key to his endurance and patience.

I certainly have felt the way Job must have. When I have been falsely accused by the enemy, I have asked, "What did I do to receive this devastating treatment? Where are You, God?" Yet the example of Job gives me encouragement that God always has a divine reason for my trials, and He wants to prove my future to my enemy, and even to myself.

Indeed we all can relate to Job. All of us, especially during loss, economic crisis or seemingly hopeless situations, are tempted to focus on the crisis. Yet if we can remain steadfast in our faith, as Job did, then our hearts will become even more connected to the Lord. God is determined to prove to the devil that even if we face loss, we will serve Him. And even more than that, He wants to prove to *us* that He will provide in famine and empower us to move beyond the crisis into a higher level of worship.

As we examine this righteous man's Accuser, let's consider some of the tactics of our adversary, which are displayed throughout God's Word.

THE ACCUSER IN THE BOOK OF MICAH

The book of Micah presents quite a contrasting picture of God's court and the Accuser that Job faced. In the book of Job, God calls Satan the "Accuser." Yet in Micah it is the Lord Himself who actually is the Accuser. But He is a different kind of Accuser altogether: He is the *Accuser of sin* with the desire to restore.

In Micah, it is Judah's day in God's court. God examines the sins of His people and righteously accuses them, yet provides an out: the blood of Jesus, which was shed to defeat sin and all false accusations. Micah 7:7 says, "But as for me, I watch in hope for the LORD, I wait for God my Savior; my God will hear me." I love this verse because it empowers me to wait on God whenever I am experiencing a fiery trial. If I watch for Him and remain positioned in hope, then I am confident that God will hear me and deliver me. I believe Job had the same thoughts in mind during his tests.

Another passage in Micah is relevant to mention as we expose the Accuser. Micah 7:8 says that the enemy will not be allowed to "gloat" over me, referring to Satan's prideful, arrogant attitude about his ability to seduce us. The Hebrew word for *gloat* is *sameach,* which means "to rejoice over a situation."[1] How dare Satan believe he can actually gloat or rejoice in believing that he can seduce the saints into apostasy! I refuse to allow the enemy to rejoice over the fact that he could falsely accuse me. Even though I may have fallen, God will empower me to arise so that no matter what happens it is not too difficult for me to serve Him.

Micah 7:9 says that though I may have walked through darkness, perhaps even embraced a season of darkness, God will plead my case. In fact, when the enemy attempts to shame me with loss and discomfort, the Lord will reverse it and clothe the Accuser with shame (see verse 10). How awesome is our God!

ESTHER AND HER ACCUSER

Two of my favorite books of the Bible are Esther and Psalms, and I find it interesting that the Lord sandwiched Job right between two such glorious books. Though Job was written years before these two accounts, the Lord chose to insert Job's account here. Why is that? I believe He had a divine reason. Perhaps it has something to do with the way that these two servants of God stood up to their Accusers. I will write about David, the psalmist, and his confrontations with the Accuser later, but first let's do a quick study on Esther. I believe we all can relate in some way to Esther's suffering. As we observe how Esther contended with the Accuser, let's also observe how God empowered her to defeat him.

A beautiful Jewish girl who rose from obscurity to prominence, Esther was chosen to become the new queen of Persia. As she went through this process, she endured her own season of testing and wondering why. As an adopted child, she may have felt unwanted. Then she was separated from her family and taken, perhaps forcibly, with many other young women to the palace to be considered as the king's new queen. Esther had to contend with these other beautiful women in a type of beauty contest, enduring numerous inspections and a great deal of unpleasant female competition. Imagine the words spoken by other women about her to intimidate her (false accusations). Imagine the insecurity she must have felt. Esther may have felt as if at any moment she would crumble under such pressure to be and to perform. And then as if all that were not enough, she had to undergo twelve months of purification.

In one of my recent books, *Destiny Thieves: Defeat Seducing Spirits and Achieve Your Purpose in God,*[2] I describe the twelve-month purification process Esther was required to endure before she was chosen queen:

> Esther did not suddenly arrive at destiny. The biblical account of Esther describes how she endured much preparation and then opposition as she pursued destiny. In preparation for marriage, Esther was anointed step by step. It was customary to deeply cleanse, purify and anoint the female body in preparation for her intimate intercession and relationship with her husband. Esther was bathed in exotic and expensive oils. . . . Esther was purified with myrrh for six months. The number six is symbolic for flesh or for man. We can conclude that Esther was purified and cleansed from all fleshly desires

and sinful nature. This was the process of perfection needed to empower her to become a queen who would shift governments and institute godly decrees. She [Esther] was not simply oiled down or sprayed with perfume like today. Rather *myrrh* was scrubbed into her skin to become a part of her—so that she herself became a sweet-smelling fragrance.[3]

Esther was being positioned not by man but by God Himself. Though she may not have known it at the time, the Lord had future plans for her, her family and her Jewish nation. Esther was called to the kingdom (and the Kingdom) "for such a time as this" to shift and reverse ungodly decrees of death. She was used by God to defeat Haman, the Amalekite (an ancient enemy of the Jews), who sought to destroy the entire Jewish race. She possibly did not even equate Haman with Satan, the Accuser. Yet it was Satan working through Haman to falsely accuse Mordecai and the Jews, even to the point of convincing King Artaxerxes to destroy all Jews in Persia. Esther passed some of the most difficult tests in life: death, rejection, abandonment, fear, betrayal and false accusations. And eventually she was established in governmental authority to reverse death decrees against her people. Thank God for Esther.

And thank God for you. In the same way He empowered Esther, God desires to empower you to defeat your false Accuser.

The symbolism attached to *myrrh* is meaningful as we contend with the Accuser:

1. Myrrh was sacred oil used to anoint the robes of the priesthood. The priests were set apart. Similarly, we too are "set apart" and anointed to serve as priests.

2. Myrrh translates as "bitter." Esther had been adopted by her cousin, Mordecai. Children with no parents often develop an orphan spirit that struggles with issues of rejection and abandonment. As Esther was scrubbed

with myrrh, her bitterness was cleansed from her life. We cannot remain bitter and move forward into destiny.

3. Myrrh was used in burial preparation. Esther had to die to self and selfish ambition to achieve the fullness of destiny. So must we.

The book of Esther empowers us with courage to face challenges and press through demonic forces that attempt to steal our future. As we face the same Accuser she faced, we must consider our own personal destinies and the ways in which we affect the lives of others. Knowing that the Accuser relentlessly seeks to defeat us also will empower us to go to the Lord for more cleansing. Dying to self and binding up all pride empowers us to defeat the Accuser.

Interestingly, God's name is not mentioned once in the account of Esther. Yet His hand is visible through all of her setbacks, challenges and circumstances. Nothing happens by accident when we love God and know Him intimately. Like He did with Esther and with Job, God will use the Accuser to prove to us that there is more of Him within our innermost parts than we realize.

BEGINNING TO FACE OUR ACCUSER

To *accuse* someone means to give a false testimony. In other words, the enemy speaks lies to us and tells us things totally opposite of what God would say. He and his demons send fiery darts into our minds and hearts. The apostle Paul wrote that those who are in Christ Jesus will face "all the fiery darts of the wicked" (Ephesians 6:16, KJV). The Lord wants us to know how to extinguish these flaming arrows, but He does not say that we can always avoid them. We *will* have opposition from the Accuser, and we *will* be opposed by Satan. God has promised, however, to empower us to overcome him and defeat his demonic strategies against us.

As we study the Accuser we must remain alert to words from many different demonic spirits. Satan, the Accuser, does not work alone. He appoints other demons to enforce his evil seductions. Many times when the enemy strikes, it seems as if the *hordes* of hell are loosed against us—and they are. *Horde* is a Hebrew word, *aggaph,* meaning "army."[4] Job was attacked by such a horde of accusers, and he suffered greatly. Job did not have a doctrine or theology to fall back upon; he had only his *relationship* with God. Oh, that we might have the same today when we are challenged with opposition and temptations from the Accuser!

What challenges are you facing this very day? The Accuser is a demon who slanders your reputation. He may be attempting to ruin your reputation by speaking lies to others concerning you. He may be speaking lies into your ears on a daily basis. He may be falsely accusing you with words such as:

1. You are not beautiful (handsome) enough to be chosen and have a mate.

2. You will never find true happiness.

3. You will always feel like an orphan—abandoned and unwanted.

4. You will never fulfill your destiny.

5. You are unworthy.

6. You will never measure up to God's expectations.

7. You will never measure up to man's expectations.

8. You are marked with shame and will never press beyond your past.

Do you relate to any of those lies? Perhaps you do, or perhaps the Accuser uses different lies concerning you. Either way, the Accuser has targeted your soul. Throughout this book, the Accuser and his lies for you will be exposed. Furthermore, you will be challenged to renew your mind concerning God, His love for you and the plans He has for your future. Knowing the plans of Satan will empower you to overthrow his plans, and knowing the plans of God for your life will empower you to move forward into your destiny. You will be encouraged to stand in faith as Jesus did in the wilderness when He faced His Accuser with a "proceeding word." Jesus declared to the Accuser, "Man shall not live on bread alone, but on every word that proceedeth out of the mouth of God" (Matthew 4:4, KJV).

Do not live by bread alone. Embrace the words of our Father and claim them for your life. I encourage you to stop right now and pray this prayer. Do not put it off.

Father, I realize the Accuser has targeted me and has been attempting to invade my thought life. I refuse to listen to the lies of the demon who is falsely accusing me. I use the keys of the Kingdom to bind up the enemy's words, which he speaks to me and to others. I plead the blood of Jesus over my life and my ears.

Though the enemy may attempt to take my case before the courts of heaven to prove me unfaithful, I will wait upon God to plead my case. The blood of Jesus cleanses me and frees me from the effects of the Accuser. I stand on Micah 7:7–9, which states: "But as for me, I watch in hope for the LORD, I wait for God my Savior; my God will hear me. . . . Though I have fallen, I will rise. . . . I will bear the LORD's wrath [against the Accuser who attempts to seduce me], until he pleads my case and establishes my right."

I just know that you desire to be free from your adversary. This book will reveal the eight main lies of the Accuser, the demonic force that attempts to steal your freedom and your future. Now, beloved, as you turn the page, more freedom awaits you.

Lie #1:

I WILL "COMFORT" YOU

But he knows the way that I take; when he has tested me, I will come forth as gold.

JOB 23:10

We all need a heart check every now and then. In fact, we need it more often than we realize. Well, beloved, this chapter is a heart check, and it is written with a deep burden. As we study Job's so-called comforters, I must warn you in advance: It is not an easy message to hear—or to give. As I reveal the mistakes that Job's friends made in their responses to their friend who was hurting, I will be asking you to take a look at your own responses to others who are in pain. I will be asking you to check your own attitudes and belief systems.

JOB'S FRIENDS USED THEOLOGY AGAINST HIM

Job had three friends who came to "comfort" him during his trials. They attempted to encourage Job with their theology. The term *theology* means "the study of God." It is derived from the Greek words *theos,* which means "God," and *logos,* which means "theory or reasoning" or "Word." In general terms, it is simply a study of religious faith, experience and practice.

Job's friends were judging him based upon what they had studied, or learned—what they knew about God. They had implemented their understanding, or learning, of God into their culture and practice, and they were judging Job and his situation based upon their own personal belief systems.

I have experienced personal challenges that others have tried to *theologically* explain, and certainly God has moved in ways that have challenged my own belief system and theology. In such situations I know that I and others have boxed in God. I also have judged others and their journeys based upon my own personal belief system. Lord, forgive me. Many times I have had to throw theology out the window and seek Him anew.

Job's friends did not bring him comfort. I have had similar experiences. At times when I have found myself in the midst of fiery trials, my friends would not listen to me when I needed comfort. From their mouths would flow forth Scripture that promised healing and deliverance. While there is nothing wrong with speaking the Word, I felt judged and condemned by a certain theology. All I desired was an opportunity to share my pain, not to be judged and declared sinful due to my circumstances.

Job's friends spoke truth, certainly, but they used the right words for the wrong circumstance. It would be like quoting Scripture out of context—laying out proven biblical principles that are supported throughout Scripture but applying them inaccurately to a person's situation. Job's friends were more concerned with theology than with compassion. They did not have a heart for Job or his trials. They became insistent on their belief that there was sin in Job's life. They had no conception of a God who would afflict someone who walked in complete faith and obedience. They completely misdiagnosed the crisis Job was enduring.

Meanwhile, God was doing something special in Job's life. Job was hurting and expressed his pain, yet he still maintained his integrity and his love for God. Job is an example to us, for he proves that we can experience pain, suffering and temptation and still maintain godly integrity. His doing so allowed God to prove Job's righteousness. Satan gave it all he had—a full-blown attack—yet Job remained committed to his belief that God was faithful and trustworthy. I know God must have loved saying "I told you so" to Satan.

JOB'S FRIENDS FOCUSED ON WHAT THEY SAW, NOT WHAT THEY HEARD

We must be careful not to judge someone else's journey. When I counsel I try to hear the person's pain, rather than assuming they have done something that has opened a door to the enemy. When someone is hit with adversity, we cannot automatically assume that he or she has been disobedient to God, nor can we rely on our own personal reservoirs of wisdom and personal beliefs.

Let me give you an example. I received a phone call from a precious pastor just the other day. As she poured out her pain, my mind raced forward, looking for a solution to her problem. My heart hurt for her, and I wanted to give her insight and direction. My mind immediately went to the "cause" of the problem, rather than encouraging her through the problem. I found myself looking for an open door, a time that maybe she "missed it" with God. Did she not have faith, did she make an unwise decision, was she a faithful giver? I finally said, "May I please pray for you? I will pray, and then let's wait on God a few moments and see if He speaks to us." So that is what we did. As I prayed, the Holy Spirit revealed to me that this pastor was going through a test and that the Accuser was literally beating her down with false accusations. But God wanted to encourage her to stand strong in her faith. I then was able to speak His words of comfort to her: "I will come through for you. You can depend on Me and My Word."

I then helped my friend make some financial decisions, and we discussed areas that might need some adjustment. But what if I had not sought the Lord? What if I had just pointed out some grave sin I thought she might have? If God was not pointing that out, then I would have been allowing myself to be influenced by the Accuser and falsely judging this precious woman of God.

Dear believers, we must be like Jesus who said, "As I hear, I judge" (John 5:30, KJV). Jesus taught us to look at the situation, then stop and listen to what the Father says concerning it. Only when we wait to hear from Him correctly can we speak to the situation and judge it properly.

Job's three friends judged incorrectly because they focused on what they *saw* rather than what they *heard* from the Father. Have you ever misdiagnosed a crisis in this way? Have you judged others because you did not stop and talk to the Father first? I believe we all have done these things in one way or another. And in doing so, we have bought in to the lies of the Accuser during times of testing.

Sometimes we simply need to bypass our religiosity and just let our hearts lead us. Having discernment is an asset in spiritual warfare, but love is the ultimate gift from God, and we must operate in that love. In order to fulfill our godly purpose we need discernment *and* love. We will not be able to help others unless we properly discern their situations and love them through the healing process. While the Accuser may be falsely accusing them, he also may be using us to persecute others. We must be on guard and ready to expose the plans of our Accuser.

JOB'S FRIENDS WERE MOTIVATED BY FAMILIAR SPIRITS

Rather than being godly comforters, Job's friends became his accusers. They were merely friends who were *familiar* with Job and were used by the enemy to tempt Job to turn away from God during his trials. Job's friends were motivated by "familiar spirits." A familiar spirit is exactly what it states: It is a spirit that is "familiar" with our lives. It uses our past to accuse us. Satan knows our weaknesses, and he targets those imperfections. He pushes our buttons, triggers our emotions and waits for opportunities to tempt us. He hopes that we will eventually give in to his snares, buy in to his lies and eventually become ineffective in our calling. The enemy hates us and often will use those closest to us to cause us to backslide and sin, just as he used Job's friends to falsely accuse him and God.

The familiar spirit also uses religion or legalism to gain entry into a person's life and then to accuse him. Religion and legalism are similar to a dictatorial government that allows no grace. When we are in bondage to legalism, we submit to laws and man's tradition rather than following God's Spirit—a higher law. If there is ever ground in which the enemy can sow demonic seeds, it is the soil of religion and legalism. Once the Accuser finds ground to sow his demonic influence, he moves in as a flood, overpowering the minds of people. It then becomes a demonic takeover. We see evidence of the Accuser attempting to use religion and legalism against Job through the words of his friends. They did not properly discern his trials but rather judged his trials due to the friends' own "religious" and "preconceived" standards.

The familiar spirit attempts to keep us wrapped in old, shameful garments of the past, when God wants us to be reclothed with robes of righteousness.

He has a kingly and priestly anointing for us, and our clean garments are waiting. Be determined to be like Job and receive a garment change.

We will discuss familiar spirits often throughout this book because these evil spirits desire to limit and tie us to our past failures.

FAMILIAR SPIRITS AND WITCHCRAFT

Scripture speaks of familiar spirits as those opening themselves up to divination and sorcery. King Saul, for example, sought out the witch of Endor, who operated in a spirit with which Saul would have been familiar—the spirit of Samuel, who had already died. By seeking out the witch's services, Saul was attempting to control his future. He was seeking a voice other than God's voice, and this is witchcraft, pure and simple. This type of witchcraft pulls upon the occult and seeks spirits that operate under a form of familiarity with the psychic or sorcerer. The one practicing witchcraft has an ungodly communication with evil spirits; each being familiar with one another and communicating out of this type of connection. In a way, these types of familiar spirits can work through those who are familiar with our lives if we allow them to "control" us.

Control can be a form of witchcraft if manipulation is evident. Manipulation occurs in different ways. One common method is to manipulate circumstances blatantly to get one's way. Another method is "charismatic witchcraft."

Charismatic witchcraft, also referred to as "white witchcraft," is praying for one's personal desires in an attempt to control the outcome of someone else's life. If a woman prays, for example, that a certain man will become her husband, then she is praying a controlling prayer. This is a dangerous form of prayer, and we must remain cautious when praying for personal desires. The only way to ensure that we are not involved in charismatic witchcraft is to pray God's perfect will for another person. We are always safe to simply pray God's Word over our lives and situations.

When we involve ourselves in charismatic witchcraft and manipulation, we open ourselves up to hear from familiar spirits. Even our closest friends can be open targets for familiar spirits if they attempt to manipulate our lives or express strong opinions concerning us. In essence, these are simply attempts to control our actions.

A CLOSER LOOK AT JOB'S THREE FRIENDS

Let's take a look at Job's familiar friends who allowed the Accuser to influence them in an attempt to falsely accuse Job and God. The names of Job's friends were Eliphaz, Elihu and Zophar. I believe revelation is concealed in their names concerning their personalities and how the Accuser was able to influence them in falsely accusing Job. We will look at each of these men individually, study their backgrounds and look at the ways the Accuser attempted to work through them. As we study, let's examine our own hearts to see if the Accuser is also falsely accusing us.

Eliphaz, the Temanite

Eliphaz's name means "my God is fine gold; God the strong; to whom God is strength. My precious God; God is dispenser. My God has refined."[1] Eliphaz was the friend who immediately responded to Job's sufferings with the belittling words, "Well, Job, if this were happening to me I would make an appeal to God, I would do such and such . . ." (Job 5:8–27, paraphrased). Remember that his name meant God is fine gold and is strong. Eliphaz spoke rhetorical words concerning the character of God and His faithfulness. Eliphaz quoted correctly concerning God, but he applied his theology to the wrong situation. Eliphaz also believed God would give strength.

Eliphaz missed, however, one key meaning in his name: "My God has refined." Eliphaz could relate to the "gold" of God, the promised blessings, and the strength God had given to him and had promised to others as well. He could not, however, wrap his mind around God's allowing a fiery affliction and trial. He did not comprehend the *refining* processes of God. Most of us do not choose to focus on that part of God either, but we must not deny that God is a consuming fire who will refine each of us at one time or another. During these times we must not falsely accuse God—or another person. We simply must embrace His fireball.

The Refiner's Fire

Malachi writes about the Refiner's fire that must occur in order for us to be acceptable to the Lord:

> But who can endure the day of his coming? Who can stand when he appears? For he will be like a *refiner's fire* or a launderer's soap. He will sit as a refiner and purifier of silver; He will purify the Levites and refine them like gold and silver.
>
> —MALACHI 3:2–3 (EMPHASIS MINE)

When Malachi penned this passage, the Jewish community was in a state similar to the way it was when Jesus walked the earth. The proud and self-righteous Pharisaism had supplanted all pure and true worship. The Pharisees' outward expressions of piety were distasteful to God. They had little heartfelt knowledge of God and instead had primarily head knowledge. They knew Scripture but could not relate to a person's pain. The legalistic view they held would not even allow someone to be healed on the Sabbath. Surely they were like Job's three friends, who judged others based upon theology and head knowledge.

Only a refining fire could wipe out this type of theology and false belief system concerning God and His ways. Religion cannot continue in such a fashion, as it will lead to a spiritual atmosphere of universal degeneracy. We must press in to present truth, a spiritual reality that is not based on past doctrine and religious mindsets.

Malachi tells the people of a coming Reformer. But what will be the character of this Reformer? He will come as a Refiner's fire that will refine both gold and silver. During the refining process the dross is separated from the precious metal. Christ, being the final Judge, embodied in truth and the administrator of the Gospel Kingdom, subjects our world to this fiery test. Only in this way is the weakness of our corrupted belief system exposed so that we can truly judge properly the ways of our God. Put simply, God will purify our minds and mindsets with his Refiner's fire.

The instant God turns up the heat, the Accuser shows up. He appears in many forms. First, he tempts us to curse God and blame Him for our hardships. The Accuser desires to bring trials and temptations that cause us to turn our backs on God and our callings.

Secondly, the Accuser uses friends to falsely accuse us, as he did with Job. These friends will spout Scripture and falsely judge us. In the midst of the fire the Accuser will accuse both us and God. He will say things such as:

- "You are going to die. Just give up. God is not hearing your plea to live."
- "God has abandoned you."
- "You have sinned and opened the door to this."
- "Because you have sinned you deserve what is happening to you."

Despite what the enemy would have us believe, God will never leave or forsake us. At the same time, He also promises to perfect (mature) us. He purposefully allows the fire to perfect us and our relationship with Him. We will, therefore, never be removed from His holy fire. Acts 2:3–4 documents the tongues of fire that lit a fresh passion upon God's people. God wants us passionate—therefore, the fire. Let's be content living in a holy furnace of fire. If we can do this, then the Accuser will never have entrance into our lives.

We can receive a supernatural grace to persevere in faithfulness—as Job did—and to be more like Jesus. Scripture testifies, "Fire goes before Him" (Psalm 97:3). This means that if we feel the fire, then we are to get excited because Jesus is coming to us in a unique way to reveal Himself. The fire is the prelude for His presence.

Buying Purified Gold

We can receive our purification from the Lord in two different ways. First, some things are simply given to us as gifts from God. Eternal life is one of those gifts that comes freely.

There are, on the other hand, things in God's Kingdom that have a price tag attached. We must buy them. Jesus refers to this in Revelation 3:18 when He states, "I counsel you to *buy* from me gold refined in the fire, that you can become rich" (emphasis mine).

I have studied this passage for years, asking for insight. The answers are in 1 Peter 1:7 and Job 23:10. Let's look at these two revelatory passages. First Peter 1:7 says,

> That the genuineness of your faith, being much more precious than gold that perishes, though it is tested by fire, may be found to praise, honor and glory at the revelation of Christ.

The treasure, the gold, is our faith, which is purified in the fire. In other words, the fire is meant to purify our faith in God as well as our faith in ourselves as we endure the fire. Remember that God allowed the Accuser to test Job to prove Job was faithful—but also to prove to Job what was in him.

Job 23:10 states, "But he knows the way that I take; when he has tested me, I will come forth as gold."

Job recognized that he needed to come forth as gold through the fiery trial. He understood the need to maintain his integrity. It is the same for us today, yet we are to embrace the need to become more *Christlike*. If we endure the fire and remain faithful, keeping growth toward Christlikeness as our ultimate goal, then we will gain the true riches of the Kingdom.

This is the true gold that is *bought*. Yes, we must pay the price, and that price is to lay down our lives and allow the Refiner to do what He does best. This particular kind of gold seems to me to be the most valuable because we pay a high price to obtain it—the price of our lives.

This gold is bought through all of our afflictions, difficulties, calamities, infirmities and other types of trials. In all of these things the Accuser will come—we can be assured of that—and he will attempt to make us bow down to his words concerning our sin and God's alleged lack of faithfulness. When trials come like these, we realize that we are out of control and that it is a good thing when God has His finger on those control issues. All we are empowered to do during these tough seasons is to respond properly—just as Job did. We can either give up and give in to the Accuser or "go for the gold." Dear ones, do not give up. Do not bow down. Instead, embrace His fire and declare, "Devil, get away from me. You are a liar. I am determined to trust God with my entire being. At the end of this fiery trial, I will be more like Jesus." And you will. I promise—even better, God promises—that at the end of the trial you will be more empowered than ever before.

Bildad

The next of Job's friends is *Bildad,* whose name means "son of contention." His name is connected to Lord Adad, the god of the Syrians. His name also translates as "confusing (by mingling) love."[2] Bildad's name implies worship in a twisted form. We see in the book of Job that Bildad attempted to confuse Job and to contend with him. In the same way, the Accuser often confuses us as to how to pray. When we are confused and uncertain, we tend to revert to old methods and patterns of prayer, when God may be trying to move us forward with fresh revelation. And if we don't move forward with the plans and purposes of God, then we will continue to contend with our enemy.

Remember that Bildad was named for a Syrian god. The word *Syrian* is rooted in the word *tsuwr* and means "to cramp and to confine."[3] Job's second "comforter" came to him with legitimate concerns but relied on a Syrian falsehood based on legalism and fabrications. Furthermore, the word *tsuwr* is related to the word for "adversary, assault, besiege, bind (up), distress, lay siege and put up in bags."[4] The spirit associated with Bildad, then, attempted to lay siege to Job and then confine Job's relationship with God.

In the same way, theology and religion can do the same to us if we are not on guard. The Accuser will take any situation and use it against us. He attempts to lay siege to us, bag us up and even suffocate us if we are not careful. We must learn to lead with our hearts and not our heads. We must not lend an ear to familiarity during uncertain times. When anything challenges our theology, we must remain on the alert.

Finally, this second friend of Job's was from the city of Bildad, an area known for its wealth and blessings. His parents probably named him after their hometown because of what it would have meant to the family heritage. His parents most likely believed that he was an incredible blessing to them—and to others. Because of this, Bildad may have considered that what he had to say was a "wealth" of information. Could it be that he had a smidgen of pride? When he spoke, did he expect people to listen? It would seem so. Bildad proved to possess a haughty attitude with his legalistic views.

Zophar

The third friend of Job was *Zophar*. His name means "choking; insolence; chatterer." This familiar spirit continually attempts to whisper lies into our ears. I know that the enemy constantly chatters into my ears when I am in the midst of a trial, and I will bet you can relate to that kind of warfare. At the same time, we can feel a choking sensation, as if we cannot breathe. That is the Accuser—the one who tries to bag us up and suffocate us. The enemy desires to choke the life out of each one of us. I am reminded of the parable of the sower in Matthew 13:22 and how the enemy will use the cares of the world to tempt us into doubt and unbelief, suffocating and choking out God's Truth:

> As for what was sown among thorns, this is he who hears the Word, but the cares of the world and the pleasure and delight and glamour and deceitfulness of riches *choke and suffocate the Word,* and it yields no fruit.
>
> —MATTHEW 13:22, AMP (EMPHASIS MINE)

The enemy wants our hearts to be seeded with thorns. Thorns are areas of pain and sorrow. When seeds of God's truth are sown into thorny hearts, the thorns will choke out the life of the seed. Thorns will suffocate any life-giving qualities a seed has to give.

We all have past pain, but we cannot allow the Accuser to continue to falsely accuse us of our past. Trauma will attempt to remain in the soil of our hearts. The enemy uses trauma to stifle us and keep us from cycling out into a healed place. The Accuser will rehearse your pain over and over and over until all truth is suffocated from your heart.

The way to defeat the Accuser in these thorny situations is to begin to speak Scriptures that declare that you are healed from past pain and trauma. The enemy has attempted to confine you with false belief systems, and the Lord wants you free.

DEMONIC WORDS AND THE KEYS TO WARFARE

If you listen to the Accuser, then you fall into sin and unbelief. Has Satan sent a vehement wind of accusations against you? Or are you hearing him blow lies like a gentle whisper of familiarity into your ears? Satan is familiar with your weaknesses and will breathe his breath of death into your thought patterns and ears.

Perhaps you can identify with these words from the Accuser:

- "God does not really care about your circumstance. You do not need to worship a God who allows you to suffer." (At this point, you begin to blame God, falsely accusing Him for your circumstances.)

- "God does not truly consider you His son/daughter." (At this point, you believe God has abandoned you.)

- "Those promises in the Bible are not for you. The promises and miracles that Jesus performed were for those during His lifetime on earth. Miracles ceased in the New Testament times." (At this point, you believe God does not desire to give you a miracle. Once more, you consider yourself "less than" or unworthy.)

- "You will never be able to be free. You have addictions and God has no desire to deliver you." (At this point, you believe God has completely abandoned you during your trials.)

- "You have sinned and therefore deserve to be condemned with sickness, disease and bondage." (At this point, you are hopeless and have lost vision for your future.)

- "God has bigger problems to solve. Your situation is unworthy of His time." (Now, you begin to experience great measures of hope deferred.)

- "Your prayers will not be answered. Do not waste your time petitioning God." (Now you will not even bother to pray. Unbelief has captivated your faith.)

Believers, God has given us the keys of heaven to bind up the wind of Satan. One of our keys for warfare involves declaring that what is in heaven is also on earth.

Jesus taught His disciples how to pray. Most of us know this prayer, but let's look at it again for more clarity:

> After this manner therefore pray ye: Our Father which art in heaven, Hallowed be thy name. Thy kingdom come, Thy will be done in earth, as it is in heaven. Give us this day our daily bread. And forgive us our debts, as we forgive our debtors. And lead us not into temptation, but deliver us from evil: For thine is the kingdom, and the power, and the glory, for ever. Amen.
>
> —MATTHEW 6:9–13, KJV

Jesus taught us to pray that what is in heaven will come to earth. There is no sickness in heaven, so it does not belong on earth. There is no poverty in heaven, so we are to petition God to release us from Satan's captivity. Jesus also taught us to pray that we would be *delivered from temptation and evil.* He did not say that we would never have to battle the Accuser who tempts us to doubt God's ability to restore, heal and deliver. When we pray, therefore, we are *binding* the devil and his false accusations.

We can never totally destroy Satan. Only God can do that, and He will do so in the final days of Revelation. We can, however, defeat him to a certain degree as we pull down strongholds and thwart his demonically inspired strategies through prayer, godly decrees and prophetic declarations. In other words, while we cannot prevent the enemy's fiery darts from coming, we can quench—or extinguish—them.

We must guard against becoming discouraged if we are under attack periodically. The Accuser wants us to back off and accept his lies; he therefore will keep hurling his fiery darts. Jesus Himself was under constant attack and scrutiny, so let's lift our heads and be proud if we have the enemy's attention. And let's remain empowered to keep the flames from consuming our perseverance and our passion.

NEGATE THE ACCUSER

Are you in the fire now? Is the Accuser falsely accusing you and God in the midst of this fiery trial? If so, grab a pen or pencil and take a few moments and document your thoughts and feelings. Use the space below to get started, but ultimately you may desire to purchase a journal to use along the way. I have written a few questions to prompt your thoughts. You can begin to negate the Accuser's words right now.

1. In the midst of pain, sorrow or trauma you have experienced, has the Accuser approached you with lies? Has he condemned and falsely accused you with words opposite of what God says concerning you, saying such things as, "It is your fault" or "You deserve to suffer because you are unworthy of healing"? Maybe he says to you, "Your life is a miserable testimony. God does not love you." Dear ones, God's love is unconditional. He loves you with an everlasting love. There is nothing you could possibly do that would cause His love to cease. If the Accuser is negating your integrity as a believer, take a

few moments and write down the lies the enemy has
been speaking to you.

2. During your trial, has the Accuser come with his
   seductive words to cause you to blame God or turn from
   Him? Is he negating how much God loves you? Write
   down the Accuser's false accusations concerning God.

3. Now take some time to locate Scriptures that negate
   the lies of the Accuser. This is important because what
   you write becomes a decree against your adversary. Do
   not pass an opportunity to agree with God's Word. Do
   not allow the Accuser to suffocate the seed of life. Your

thorny soil will become purified by His Word, and you will experience His life-giving power and love as you write. A window in heaven has opened, and heaven awaits your decree. God is waiting for you to speak His Words concerning your life. When you decree a thing, it is therefore established (see Job 22:28). The Lord is promising you that He will watch over His Word to perform it (see Jeremiah 1:12). Remember: It is your season to be free.

I would like to pray for you now. Let's agree together that you are advancing forward into great breakthrough.

Father, let us always stop and hear from You. Though we may be in the fire, we know that You are determined to perform Your perfect work in us. We want to embrace this fiery trial and buy gold from You. We desire that our faith be purified and that we are more Christlike. We will not listen to the voice of the Accuser but rather be determined to know You more.

I pray for each reader as he or she continues on a journey through this book. As this dear one reads and studies, I ask that You come closer. I know that every believer has experienced your holy fire, but I ask for abundant grace as they continue to move forward in understanding Your perfect love. I bind up the Accuser in the name of Jesus and command him to be silenced as Your child learns to walk in freedom. I pray that the decrees of this believer will touch heaven and manifest in the earth. I thank You in advance for opening up windows of heaven as each reader confesses breakthrough.

In Jesus' name, Amen.

3

Lie #2:
SHAME ON YOU

We are more than conquerors through him who loved us. . . .
I am convinced that neither death nor life, neither angels nor
demons, neither the present nor the future, nor any powers, nei-
ther height nor depth, nor anything else in all creation, will be
able to separate us from the love of God that is in Christ Jesus our
Lord.

ROMANS 8:37–39

Rachab had always been rather quiet and withdrawn. She was one of those unfortunates who always looked for love in all the wrong places. She always sought fulfillment yet never experienced it. Her life was out of control. She was compelled to sin and yet at the same time blamed herself for her past.

Satan, the Accuser, relentlessly spoke lies to Rachab's mind with words such as, "You are worthless. No one loves you. You are a sinner. God Himself does not even love you. Even your name is derived from Rahab, the prostitute. You are from a lineage of evil, sinful, lustful women. There is no hope for you ever to be more than garbage to society. No man can ever truly love you." The Accuser's words stung day after day.

Rachab's emotions were at toxic levels. She fought feelings of hopelessness, despair, rejection, depression and anxiety. *Why can't I control my pain?* The question raced consistently through her mind. Rachab had come to the end of her rope and was left sobbing each night. She desired to cycle out of her anguish.

God, if You are real, prove that You love me. Rachab would fall asleep each night with this prayer of desperation in her heart.

The Accuser was right about one thing: Her name was rooted in Rahab's name. Yet Rahab, the prostitute of the Old Testament who saved the lives of Joshua and Caleb, ultimately cycled out of her shame and became a grandmother to King David and an ancestor of Jesus Himself. Scripture honors her as a righteous woman of faith because of what she did for the two spies in Jericho (see Hebrews 11:31 and James 2:25). Rachab's parents had specifically chosen her name because they believed that, like Rahab, she was a gift to God and others. Her name meant "to broaden (as in horizons), to (become or make) enlarged, to make room and to make (open wide)."[1] They prayed she would have a gift of love and walk confidently in the covenant of Jehovah, that she would dream big and enter open doors of greatness. Her parents' hearts had been flooded with hopes for their daughter's future, yet when Rachab was quite young, both parents died prematurely. With no other family to take her in, Satan saw his chance.

Rachab was forced to sell her body for survival. When she could find a man to care for her, she stayed until he tired of her. Any hopes of truly being a wife, experiencing pure godly, emotional intimacy with a man, seemed hopeless to someone like Rachab.

The Accuser was determined to cause Rachab to fail in life so that she would never be able to fulfill her potential and glorify God.

The Accuser always marks those with potential and then attempts to steal it. He continually twisted the truth to falsely accuse Rachab, whom God considered blessed. He took her weaknesses and magnified them with lies, convincing her she was unworthy of God's love.

Believing the Accuser, Rachab spent most of her days alone. Ashamed to venture too far into the marketplace, she waited for attention at night. The warmth of a man's touch seemed to give her a level of validity—but only for a short while. The hope of finding true love paled against her deep-seated rejection. Each morning she would awaken alone to another guilt-ridden day, emotionally and spiritually unsatisfied. Her shame clothed her, blocking any chances of anyone really knowing her. Rachab was a slave to her past.

One of these lonely mornings, Rachab puttered around outdoors while her mind wandered again. *Why did I meet that man again last night? I know he is married and is just using me.* She strolled down a narrow walkway, carefully studying the rough stones along the path. *I am like those stones,* she thought, *sharp, unhoned edges upon which men walk.* A tear rolled down her cheek.

Feeling totally hopeless, she turned around and went back to the house of her lover. She softly knocked on the door, and he answered. "Are you alone? I need to spend some time with you. Is your wife here?" He drew her inside.

Suddenly she felt an instant jerk. Her arms were thrust forward and bound. "Let me go! Let me go!" Thrown to the floor, her lover was stunned. Rachab was taken captive and dragged to the streets by her captors. *What is happening to me? Who are these men who are saying such terrible things and hurting me?* She felt a silent scream deep within her, though she could utter no sound.

In the courts of the Temple, Jesus turned at the harsh voice calling, "Make way! Make way!" All of those in the large crowd who had been listening to His teaching turned their heads, too, to see what caused the commotion.

The scribes and Pharisees brought Rachab to Jesus and made her stand in the middle of the court. One man spoke up and told Jesus,

> Teacher, . . . this woman has been caught in the very act of adultery. Now Moses in the Law commanded us that such [women, offenders] shall be stoned to death. But, what do You say?
>
> JOHN 8:4–5, AMP

Rachab stood with her head down. She could not look up at anyone. According to the Law, only a betrothed virgin could be stoned to death, including guilty parties. Yet the crowd obviously considered her worthy of stoning, and she was convinced that she deserved to die. She even *wanted* to die. She felt it would be a relief from her tortuous pain to be punished for her crime.

Jesus knew that the accusations against her were a type of *testing* meant for Him. The religious accusers were seeking a charge to actually accuse not only Rachab, but also to falsely accuse Jesus. The Pharisees had been looking for an opportunity to arrest Jesus, and they used the sins of Rachab to see if Jesus would judge her appropriately by their interpretation of the Law. They were attempting to trap Jesus and prove that He was not a teacher from God. The religious leaders were persistently seeking to quarrel with Jesus to ensnare Him. The Accuser was working relentlessly to falsely accuse Jesus, in addition to Rachab.

The Pharisees hurled questions at Jesus again. "What is Your judgment? We should stone her. What do You say?"

Jesus stooped over from where He was sitting and began to write on the ground with His finger. The crowd quieted as it waited to see what He was doing. Then Jesus stood up and said, "Let him who is without sin among you be the first to throw a stone at her."

Then, He bent down and continued writing on the ground with His finger (see John 8:7–8).

The finger of Jesus was anointed. Luke 11:20 says, "But if I by the finger of God cast out demons, then is the Kingdom of God come upon you" (ASV). Jesus' finger ushered God's Kingdom into the situation. He knew that He was defeating Satan, the Accuser, that day and that Rachab's life would be forever saved and changed.

One by one the crowd dissipated. The accusers who clutched stones dropped them and left, conscience-stricken, one by one. No one was without sin—and they knew it. Jesus was left alone with Rachab standing before Him in the center of the court.

Jesus stood back up and looked tenderly at Rachab. "Woman, where are your accusers? Is there anyone here to condemn you now?"

Rachab was stunned, overwhelmed and shaking. She took a deep breath, still not understanding all that had just taken place. She looked at Jesus, and respectfully answered Him, "No one, Lord."

"Neither do I condemn you. Go on your way, and do not sin again." Jesus knew that when someone sins, he is a slave to sin. Jesus did not desire that Rachab remain in bondage, so He instructed her to sin no more.

Broken, brought to repentance and forgiven, Rachab walked away a changed woman. She felt God's love for the first time—but it was more than love. It was a divine enablement to sin no more. Rachab was forever changed. She was not simply set free; she was *free indeed.*

LIGHTING UP THE ACCUSER'S DARKNESS

This is the biblical account of a woman who had forfeited her moral integrity and committed a shameful sin, yet met Jesus and was forgiven (see John 8). While I have taken a bit of liberty with this story, expanding upon it a bit and actually naming the woman, who is unnamed in the biblical account, it is a true story and one to which we all can relate in some way or another.

Female or male, we all have messed up. Whether we have engaged in the sin of adultery, homosexuality or any other type of sexual perversion, or any other type of sin, we live with the resulting shame of that sin. Jesus wants to release all of us from condemnation and accusation.

Scripture goes on to say that when the woman was released, Jesus turned once more and addressed the crowd. Jesus confronted the darkness that accompanies the Accuser, pronouncing, "I am the Light of the world. He who follows Me will not be walking in the dark, but will have the Light which is Life" (John 8:12, AMP).

Jesus was testifying that the Accuser is the author of darkness and brings only death. Satan, who falsely accuses his victims, attempts to steal life and hope. He is a liar and a murderer. John 8:44 states that the devil is "a murderer from the beginning, and does not stand in the truth, because there is no truth in him" (AMP). John goes on to write that Satan is the father of lies and of all that is false. Even as He spoke that day, Jesus was exposing the Accuser, shining light onto the darkness of Satan's lies.

Knowing Satan is a liar, why do we listen to him? Because he is also the Accuser. He twists the truth and seduces us to believe that all that goes wrong is our fault. He wants us to blame ourselves, rather than bind him and his evil works. He hates repentance and therefore keeps us in a guilt and shame cycle, convincing us we are too unworthy to receive God's forgiveness. The Accuser prides himself in keeping believers on an emotional merry-go-round that never cycles out of the wilderness.

The Accuser falsely testifies (speak lies into our ears) and attempts to bring judgment when we sin. He tells us we have to be punished. This is not true, for Jesus died and shed His blood so that we are forgiven. He took our punishment for us. I am, of course, not advocating that we should willfully sin. What I mean is that if we do sin, we are already forgiven. We still need to appropriate His forgiveness as we repent (turn) from the sin, but we also must realize that Christ died so that we are free from punishment.

The accused woman was caught "in the act" of adultery and deserved a level of punishment for her sin, but Christ set her free. It is the same with each of us. We sin, but Christ died so that we are forgiven and set free.

Have you allowed the enemy to falsely accuse you and cause you to feel unworthy of God's love and salvation? Are you hurting in any way and feel as if God has forgotten you? Most of us have pain. God is the best pain reliever you will ever find. If you will believe God to forgive you, then you will be amazed how much emotional pain will flee. God desires to release you from the pain of your past. It's simple, really, to receive salvation and forgiveness. Simply ask Him (Jesus) into your heart. I believe the woman of ill repute received Him into her heart the moment He addressed the Accuser on her behalf.

Jesus shone light on the darkness that consumed the woman's life. Could we possibly receive the same type of response from Jesus when the Accuser torments us? Absolutely.

SHAME HOLDS US CAPTIVE

"Shame on you." It is a phrase often used by the Accuser. Shame is so familiar to most of us that we often do not realize that we embrace it so easily.

Looking back over my own life, I now recognize the shame patterns that held me captive. I remember being in high school and being rejected by my peers. I came from a relatively affluent family, so the shame I felt was not because of poverty. My shame was rooted in the false belief that I never measured up to others. I was performance-oriented; I had to fulfill tasks and please everyone in order to have self-worth.

I am a small person, only a smidgen away from five feet three inches. I desperately wanted, however, to be a basketball player. I know—I should have chosen a different sport on which to focus (which I later did), but I absolutely loved playing basketball. Somehow I made the "A Team," probably because I was a "scrapper." I was fast and determined to outthink others. I could steal the ball before anyone knew it was gone and pass the ball quickly to a forward to score the points.

The other team members, however, made fun of me because I was so short and was playing guard—a position usually reserved for the tall girls. Their ridicule hurt deeply. I felt rejected by my peers, even though I had an active life as a basketball player and cheerleader and in several other sports.

My mother had been an All-Star State Championship basketball player. She also was beautiful and sang like an angel. (I sing also, by the way. My mother coached me in singing from the age of three.) After my parents would come to my basketball games, Mom would compare how she had formerly maneuvered the ball and would give me coaching instructions. I believe her motive was to empower me, but I felt that I could not measure up to her expectations. The harder I tried to please her, the worse I played. I would stumble and fall facedown on the court when she would come. I was so nervous that I could not do anything right.

Eventually, the emotional pain grew so intense that I quit the basketball team. I cried the day I turned in my suit because I loved the game so much. But the shame I felt for not measuring up to certain standards from my parents and the other team members became so painful that I simply could not continue.

The Accuser uses shame to his advantage as he seeks to destroy us. Once we embrace shame, we cannot believe what God says about us; we believe the opposite. I embraced my shame, and it continued to grow and permeate many other areas of my life.

In my book *Dream On: Unlocking Your Dreams and Visions*,[2] I explain the demonic assignments that were exposed during years of godly dreams. Through dreams, the Lord showed me generational patterns and strongholds from my childhood that bound me. God healed and delivered me from many demons that were attached to trauma, sexual abuse, fear, anxiety, anorexia and bulimia. Many dreams revealed strong generational iniquities (or assignments) that were passed from previous family members, intentionally or unintentionally. Through the years of much emotional healing, I have realized that shame was a root problem, and God's axe was being laid to it to bring freedom and healing.

One thing I began to realize were the many repetitive and *twisted* thought patterns to which I was bound. I had bought in to Satan's lies. "You will never be good enough." "You will never be thin enough." "You are not smart enough." "Shame on you." For the first thirty years of my life I battled self-rejection, self-hatred and low self-esteem. Deep down, I truly believed that I was flawed. No matter how hard I tried, I never felt good enough or worthy enough to receive love—especially God's love. I could not allow myself to make a mistake; even the minutest mistake sent me into a tailspin. To make any mistake at all meant I was a failure.

I grew angrier with myself each time I messed up. The Accuser replayed my mistakes over and over until I would finally surrender and believe that I was shameful. The root problem was not that I might make a mistake. I believed I was the mistake. Can you relate? When we believe these lies, shame becomes our identity.

When I recovered physically from anorexia and bulimia, the Accuser convinced me that I deserved to die because I had sinned and should be punished. Despite getting down to a weight of only 78 pounds, I had survived the illness with no permanent damage.

That alone was a miracle. (My entire testimony is told in *Dream On.*) Though I was healed, the Accuser began to lie to me that God was going to punish me for my sin. And I believed him.

Then when I was 35 years old, I developed a terminal blood infection—a truly horrendous illness. I was completely overwhelmed in the spiritual battle against death. I began to dream about my funeral. I would awaken in the middle of the night in a cold sweat, and a demon (the spirit of death) would manifest. I recognized the demon immediately and knew he was after me. The Accuser bombarded me with death threats. He taunted me with words such as, "Your God does not love you. You deserve to die. Do not waste your time praying for God to heal you. God has judged you guilty." The enemy seduced me into believing his lies of death and destruction.

I had developed an ungodly belief system that was rooted in shame. Shame opened the door to the anorexic behavior, and while I had been healed of anorexia, I was not rid of the shame. Shame literally almost destroyed me.

CREATED IN GOD'S IMAGE

So how can we cycle out of this false belief system that embraces shame? The only way to defeat the Accuser and put shame under our feet is to believe the basic truth that each of us is created in God's image.

In the Garden of Eden, God did not put any conditions upon Adam and Eve except not to eat from one tree. He did not instruct them to measure up or weed the Garden with excellence. He did not label them worthless, ugly, fat or thin. Rather, He made them in His own image and blessed them, even giving them power and dominion (see Genesis 1:26–31).

The word *image* in this passage is the Hebrew word *tselem*, which means "resemblance," but it is from a root word meaning "to shade."[3]

Barnes' Notes connects the word image with God's "likeness."[4] The word *likeness* is the Hebrew word *demuwth,* which also means a resemblance, but it goes further to translate it as "being concretely (made or modeled)."[5] In other words, when God made man, He did so to the degree that we are "concretely" created like Him. We have a covenant relationship with God, but to remain in the covenant protection we must not come into covenant with the lies of the enemy.

When we are concretely created in His image, then His glory "shades" us or covers us. When we realize who we are in Christ and that we are created to be like Him, then we can visualize ourselves *concretely set* in who He is and take cover in His glory.

God created all things and saw that it was *good.* The word *good* is a Hebrew word *towb,* which translates as good in the widest sense; it "encompasses all that is pleasing, well, beautiful, cheerful, having favour, joyful, kind, merry, most pleasant, pleasurable, precious, prosperous, sweet, wealthy and well-favored."[6] God says we are "good." To Him, we are all of these things. We are not bad people. We are not defeated, worthless and hopeless. We are beautiful beings who are created in His image.

God looks upon us and sees what He fashioned. So why don't we see the same thing?

The answer is that the Accuser is working overtime. He lies and tells us that we are not blessed, not good, not created in God's image. If we buy in to this, then we are left feeling uncovered and ashamed.

Upon creation, Adam and Eve walked in total fellowship with God. His presence alone provided protection and covering. Adam and Eve were secure in who they were, for their identity was in Him. They were naked yet did not know shame because God's glory covered them. Then they chose to listen to the beguiling Accuser and sinned. Eve did not trust the fact that God knew what was best, so she opted to develop her own identity outside of God's. Then Adam did the same. After Adam and Eve sinned, they realized they were naked and became ashamed. They had not known shame until they realized they were uncovered. What uncovered them? Their sin had caused them to be uncovered. They had chosen a different identity outside of being one with God, and God's glory had left them.

But when Jesus came, He brought God's glory back to earth and offered that covering once again. He offered that covering to the woman of ill repute when He confronted her enemies and her sin. At the same time, Jesus confronted the religious system and the Accuser, and the woman was free to go. Christ's truth set her free. She saw who she was through His eyes, and it changed her life. She no longer had to carry her burden of shame.

Mary Magdalene is another example of this principle. While some believe she and the woman of ill repute are one and the same, she is not biblically referred to as the prostitute whom Jesus pardoned. The Bible is clear, however, that Jesus cast out of Mary Magdalene seven demons. Can you imagine the shame of that day? She must have felt completely humiliated and exposed. Some would have gone away feeling totally guilt-ridden and suicidal. Yet after this encounter with the Lord, Mary did not allow the shame of her past to defile her future with Christ as her deliverer. She chose Jesus as her Lord and truly persevered as she followed Him.

Dear ones, I encourage you to continue on our journey to receive complete deliverance. Do not allow the Accuser to steal your identity by seducing you to believe you are opposite of what God says about you. You do not have to live with the shame.

RUN TO THE LORD

When God puts His finger on an area of our lives to deliver us, many of us fear exposure. We feel "naked" and "ashamed." But dear ones, we must not try to hide from God. (We cannot hide from

Him anyway.) Instead we need to run to Him, admit our shame and our sin and know He is faithful to forgive us.

God's Word says that nothing—not prostitution, adultery, addictions, demons—nothing can separate us from God's desire to empower us with divine potential (see Romans 8:38). He says He will never leave us or forsake us (see Deuteronomy 31:6, 8; Joshua 1:5; 1 Kings 8:57 and Hebrews 13:5).

Yet the Accuser keeps knocking at the doors of our hearts and minds to convince us we are guilty of a crime and therefore deserve God's wrath and punishment. Believing these lies spirals us downward, and we fall into our Accuser's trap. He wants us to accept his lies and remain in shame. He reminds us of the further shame that would come if we were to admit our sin and seek counsel. We must keep in mind that we cannot keep dark secrets without even *more* shame covering us.

Don't fall into the trap of the Accuser. I encourage you to run to your Lord God. Confess your sin now—and rid yourself of shame. Just as Jesus chose to forgive a woman who had committed a sin that demanded punishment by law, Jesus waits to forgive you, too. The Accuser always demands punishment, yet Jesus came to destroy this Pharisee mentality and to set us free from the Accuser. Though we may be guilty of sin, Jesus removed the guilt, shame and punishment when He nailed our sins to the cross. He became sin for us.

Be tenacious, as Rachab was. Rebuke the Accuser and remove the false covering of shame. Salvation and freedom await you.

IDENTIFYING AND REBUKING YOUR ACCUSER

1. Can you identify any areas of toxic shame that attempt to remain as a false covering over you?

2. Can you identify the words of the Accuser that bring you shame? (They may sound like your own thoughts.)

3. Do you feel as if you deserve punishment for your past sin?

4. Now look up the following verses in your Bible and rebuke your Accuser.

   a. Read Genesis 1:26–31. Think of the details that went into creating Adam and Eve. They are the same details that God invested in you. God concretely created you in His image.

   b. Read Psalm 139:11–17. God created you in His image, and He covered you even while you were in your mother's womb.

   c. Read John 1:12 and Galatians 3:26. You are a child of God.

   d. Read Philippians 4:13. You can do all things—even defeat the Accuser.

   e. Read Colossians 2:9–10. You are complete in Him and delivered from all shame.

   f. Read Zechariah 2:8. Declare that the devil cannot touch you, for you are the apple of God's eye.

   g. Read Psalm 91. You are abiding under the shadow of His wings. God is your high tower and your fortress.

Dear reader, God has a garment change for you. Yes, God desires to remove the garments (with those ungodly labels) of your shame and give you fresh, anointed garments to empower you for the future. I want you to see yourself fully clothed in God's glory. May I pray for you?

> *God, You are awesome. Thank You that You created my dear reader with purpose and destiny. Thank You that he/she does not have to live with shame. Thank You that through His redeeming work on the cross Your precious Son made the way for this precious child of Yours to throw off the old garments of shame and put on the new man. Thank You that You cover us. In Jesus' name, Amen.*

Dear one, "Put on the new man that is being renewed unto knowledge after the image of Him that created him" (Colossians 3:10, ASV).

Now, where are your accusers?

4

Lie #3:
LISTEN TO MY WHISPERS

*Then he showed me Joshua the high priest standing before
the angel of the LORD, and Satan standing at his right side to
accuse him.*

ZECHARIAH 3:1

Zechariah 3:1–2 speaks of Satan standing *right beside* the high priest.
That is really too close for comfort.

Indeed, the devil wants to be that close to us. He wants us to
become *comfortable* and *familiar* with his lies. Reader, let me be
blunt: If you are a believer, then not only is the enemy trying to
stand beside you to falsely accuse you, but he also is attempting
to come even closer. Yes, he wants to get close enough to *whisper*
into your ears.

If the devil is whispering into your ears, then he is way too close.
In fact, if you are not careful, you might even become comfortable

with his being there. When that happens, his voice becomes familiar—sometimes even more familiar than the voice of the Lord.

WHISPERS AND INTIMACY

A whisper is really an intimate act. I love it when my husband whispers into my ear. He can be a cuddler when he wants to be. His whispers show his attentiveness and affection and are a sign of our intimacy.

With whom do you whisper? I am sure it is only with those who are closest to you.

Now consider this: Are you listening to the whispers of the Accuser? If you are, you can hear him only because he is able to be close to you. You have allowed him close proximity. You have allowed him access to your life. You are being intimate with him. Is he the one with whom you want to be intimate?

My husband is also protective and has at times whispered a correction. At a dinner table with others, for example, he has leaned in to whisper, "Sandie, watch your mouth—you are about to say something you will regret."

My husband knows me—way too well. And God knows me even better. Yet when the Lord prompts my heart with a gentle whisper, I do not always pay attention. Sometimes He has to shout because I am not close enough to Him to hear His whispers. Sometimes He has to shout even louder because I am too busy listening to the whispers of the Accuser.

If we are walking too close to the Accuser, then we are too intimate with him and we cannot hear God. We should not allow the Accuser close access. Rather, we should always walk so closely with God that we immediately hear His—and only His—whispers. We should be that intimately involved with Him.

CLOSE ENOUGH TO WHISPER

Now, I do not know about you, but I am normally cautious about whom I allow close enough to whisper to me. If it was someone I did not know or trust, he or she would not get past my personal boundary. If it was someone who was unclean, defiling or repulsive, I would run in the opposite direction.

Yet all too often I find myself listening to the Accuser's whispers. Later, when I am left feeling defiled, doubting God, confused and ashamed, I realize I allowed Satan to get too close to me. How could I allow that to happen?

At such times, either Satan caught me off guard or I allowed myself to become too familiar and comfortable with him. As a result, my mind is infected and my heart is hardening.

Can you relate? I will bet that right now your mind is racing as you are recalling the times the Accuser slyly whispered into your ears. He might have whispered:

- "If you are not perfect, no one will love you."
- "If you are not attractive enough, you will never marry."
- "If you are not successful, you will never be fulfilled."
- "Since God always promises to forgive you, go ahead and sin."
- "God does not answer *your* prayers."
- "Your needs are not important to God."
- "You will always be a victim."
- "Your addictions will always control you."
- "You are not worthy of love."

Dear one, your Accuser wants you to listen to his whispers, and they are all lies.

THE ACCUSER'S WHISPERS LEAD TO BANKRUPTCY

Bankruptcy. It is an ugly word. Most of us relate it to finances, but it also refers to *relational bankruptcy* with God. To be bankrupt is to be totally depleted and in a ruined state.

Bankruptcy is what the Accuser plans for us, God's priesthood. In Zechariah 3:1–2 Satan is at the side of the high priest, accusing him. He does the same for us, God's priesthood, today. He desires to get as close as he can to us so that he can cause a bankruptcy in our relationship with God.

Can you relate to a recent season where your faith has been exhausted? When the Accuser attacks you, your identity is challenged. Satan is relentless with his onslaughts of despair, hopelessness and torment. When you have battled the Accuser for a while, your faith feels as limp as a dishrag. Empty. Hollow. Burned-out. Completely bankrupt.

You probably have felt unstable during uncertain times. When the Accuser pointedly strikes, you feel as if you lose any sure footing you once had. It is difficult to remain standing solid on the Rock when the Accuser comes calling. The devil wants us to doubt God and His ability to provide for our needs.

Let me assure you that you are not alone. Let's take a look at one righteous man of the Bible who listened to the whispers of the Accuser and went through a time of relational bankruptcy with God but came through his wilderness experience to know a new voice of the Lord.

GOD'S WHISPER TO ELIJAH

First Kings describes how the Lord spoke to His servant Elijah with His gentle whisper:

> Then a great and powerful wind tore the mountains apart and shattered the rocks before the LORD, but the LORD was

not in the wind. After the wind there was an earthquake, but
the LORD was not in the earthquake. After the earthquake
came a fire, but the LORD was not in the fire. And after the
fire came a gentle whisper.

—1 KINGS 19:11–12

What positioned Elijah for God's whisper? Well, it was not
because Elijah remained in close contact with God all the time. In
fact, not long before he heard God's whisper, Elijah was confused,
fearful and running from God. Let's backtrack a little bit and take
a look at what was going on in Elijah's life.

In the previous chapter, 1 Kings 18, Elijah had challenged King
Ahab, Queen Jezebel and the 450 priests of Baal. The miraculous
result was that Elijah proved the priests of Baal powerless, boldly
displayed God's awesome power by calling down fire from heaven
to burn up a water-drenched sacrifice, tore down the altar of Baal,
built the altar of God and slaughtered every last one of the priests
of Baal. Elijah then prayed to the Lord to send rain to end the
drought that had covered the land, and the Lord did. Then the
power of the Lord came upon Elijah so strongly that he ran all
the way back to Jezreel ahead of King Ahab and his entourage on
their horses (and possibly chariots). What a demonstration of the
power of God, right?

You would think that after all of that Elijah would have been
completely overflowing with confidence and faith in the Lord. You
would think the prophet would have felt close to God. But a short
time later, possibly even the same day, Jezebel sent a messenger to
Elijah to threaten him: "May the gods deal with me, be it ever so
severely, if by this time tomorrow I do not make your life like that
of one of [the priests of Baal]" (1 Kings 19:2).

So what did Elijah do? He ran for his life. Can you believe it?

After such a public and powerful display of God's authority and dominion, Elijah ran away in fear.

Perhaps he was exhausted, for often when we are physically and spiritually tired we become weaker in our faith. Perhaps he was more afraid of Jezebel than Ahab. Perhaps he was just completely overwhelmed by his circumstances. But whatever the reason, when the message from Jezebel came, Elijah did not stop to ask for or listen to God's instruction. Rather, he listened to the defiling whisper of his Accuser, and he ran. And not only that: Elijah even asked God to let him die.

> When he came to Beersheba in Judah, he left his servant there, while he himself went a day's journey into the desert. He came to a broom tree, sat down under it and prayed that he might die. "I have had enough, LORD," he said. "Take my life; I am no better than my ancestors." Then he lay down under the tree and fell asleep.
>
> —1 KINGS 19:3–5

I want to pause here for a minute and take a brief look at the evil Queen Jezebel to help gain insight into why Elijah feared her so. This Old Testament queen was the embodiment of a murdering spirit of the enemy that is named for her: the spirit of Jezebel. Just like the evil queen, the spirit of Jezebel murders, falsely accuses, controls, manipulates and teams up with perversion and idolatry. In my book *Breaking the Threefold Demonic Cord: Exposing and Defeating Jezebel, Athaliah and Delilah,* I discuss the many tactics of these three seductive spirits, the most powerful of which is Jezebel. Jezebel's standard operating procedure with God's children is to continually send evil messages to seduce them into apostasy and idol worship. When she sent her evil message to Elijah concerning her desire to slay him, she was teaming up with the Accuser.

That time, her control worked. Elijah was in a weak spot, and the Accuser's evil whispers sent the prophet running in the opposite direction of his godly assignment. Jezebel's intent is the same today; she exists to issue death decrees over our lives. When she is linked with the Accuser, the spirit of Jezebel opposes after every victory.

Believers, if you get only one main point from this chapter, remember this: The Accuser's voice is deceptive, and his whispers are seductive. He will attempt to mock and sometimes counterfeit the whispers of God. Satan will wait until after a Sunday morning victory to ring the doorbell on a blue Monday. He hopes we will be tired enough, or caught off guard enough, that he can sidle up that close to us and we will open the door. And if we let him get that close, his evil whispers will cause us to run in the wrong direction and lead us to death, destruction and despair.

That is what happened to Elijah. He listened to the Accuser, and he began to wallow in despair. But God did not forget about His servant, Elijah. He sent an angel to him to comfort him and feed him—twice. Then, according to 1 Kings 19:7–13:

- Elijah got up, ate and drank and then traveled forty days and nights.

- He arrived at Mount Horeb, the mountain of the Lord, went into a cave and spent the night.

- The Word of the Lord came to him and asked, "What are you doing here, Elijah?" (verse 9)

- Elijah told God all the things he had done for the Lord, as well as his fears.

- The Lord told Elijah to prepare to go out of the cave and stand on the mountain in the presence of the Lord, for He was about to pass by.

- Still in the cave, Elijah heard a great wind that tore the mountains apart and shattered the rocks—but the Lord was not in the wind.

- Elijah then witnessed an earthquake—but the Lord was not in the earthquake.

- After that Elijah witnessed a powerful fire—but the Lord was not in the fire.

- After the fire came a gentle whisper—and the Lord was in the whisper.

- It was then that Elijah pulled his cloak over his face and came out of the cave.

We can learn several important lessons from Elijah's experience.

1. God uses everything for His good and positions His people to hear His whisper.

Though Elijah ran away from God, by the end of his journey God had drawn him closer. Dear ones, God never gives up on us. Elijah took off into a wilderness and ended up on higher ground. Mount Horeb was considered the mountain of God. It was the place where Moses had received the Ten Commandments, and it was also the mountain on which Elijah's servant, Elisha, would later receive instructions from God. So from a place of fear and lack of faith, God brought Elijah up to that mountaintop, prepared to hear His soft whisper. Indeed, God positioned Elijah for His whisper.

2. God desires to "pass by" us when we are in a cave.

The words *pass by* have their root in a Hebrew word, *abar,* which means "to cross over, to cover and to soar."[1] God first sheltered Elijah in the cave and at the appointed time called him out so that He could cover Elijah with His glory and restore him with purpose. Isn't that wonderful? In the same way, God desires to cover us with His glory, to restore us with purpose and to empower us to cross over into our future. I want to soar with God, don't you?

3. God will transform and empower us with His whisper.

God will not always sound the same. At times God does speak through a wind, fire or earthquake. But there are times, especially when we are defiled by the whisper of the Accuser, that we can be transformed, changed and empowered for our future only by God's whisper. And Elijah's time in the wilderness prepared him to hear the new sound of God. It was the Lord's still, small voice that caused Elijah to cover his face with his cloak. God's whisper must have been quite intimate for Elijah to feel led to cover himself. He was exposed to the One who sees us inside and out. Nothing is hidden from Him. If God is beckoning you closer to Him, then be encouraged and listen closely for His whisper. He is about to empower you with new vision and a refined future. God's whispers will astonish you, amaze you and cause your heart to become ablaze once again.

Elijah's experience began with a whisper—that of his Accuser—but ended with the empowering whisper of God. Through that divine whisper, Elijah was empowered by God to live—and to live for His glory. When we are challenged with false accusations and overwhelming circumstances, the Lord overrules our death wishes and transforms us once again, redirecting us toward our destiny. What an awesome God we serve!

THE WHISPERS OF WITCHCRAFT

In the book of Psalms, King David offers some practical accounts of how the enemy whispers against God's people:

> All who hate me whisper together about me; against me do they devise my hurt—imagining the worst for me. An evil disease, say they, is poured out upon him and cleaves fast to him; and now that he is bedfast, he will not rise up again. Even my own familiar friend, in whom I trusted (relied on

and was confident), who ate of my bread, has lifted up his heel against me. But do You, O Lord, be merciful and gracious to me and raise me up, that I may requite them.

—PSALM 41:7–10, AMP

This passage is relating familiar friends, evil whispers and plans for evil. The word for *whisper* in this passage is *lachash,* which is a Hebrew word meaning "to whisper, to charm and to conjure."[2] This word, therefore, is connected to sorcery, the occult and witchcraft. In other words, when someone familiar to us is used by Satan to whisper and devise plans of harm, the enemy uses his or her words as a curse of witchcraft against us. Dear ones, every time we speak evil of one another, it empowers Satan.

The prophet Isaiah also warns us about consulting those who whisper. He says that we should be forewarned never to consult gossipers or whisperers, or we will be exposed to spirits of darkness, distress and anguish (see Isaiah 8:19–22). If we consult those who "whisper," we are consulting the spirits of darkness, and Satan's occult power of evil surrounds us. Take heed, dear ones, and stay far away from the whispers of witchcraft.

POSITIONING OURSELVES FOR GOD'S WHISPER

As we prepare ourselves to face our Accuser, we must position ourselves properly. We cannot be too close to the enemy, or we might hear and listen to his whispers. We must instead make sure we are intimately close to the Lord, for it is His whispers we need to be hearing.

As we position ourselves properly for the future, we must remember two main points:

1. **God wants us to abide in Him so that we can bear fruit. Bearing fruit is like punching Satan in the stomach and**

taking all the wind out of him. Furthermore, God says we must not simply bear fruit but that we should bear fruit that will last.

> As the Father has loved me, so have I loved you. Now *remain* in my love. If you obey my commands, you will *remain* in my love, just as I have obeyed my Father's commands and *remain* in his love. I have told you this so that my joy may be in you and that your joy may be complete. My command is this: Love each other as I have loved you. Greater love has no one than this, that he lay down his life for his friends. You are my friends if you do what I command. I no longer call you servants, because a servant does not know his master's business. Instead, I have called you friends, for everything that I learned from my Father I have made known to you. You did not choose me, but I chose you and appointed you to *go and bear fruit— fruit that will last.* Then the Father will give you whatever you ask in my name. This is my command: Love each other.
>
> —JOHN 15:9–17 (EMPHASIS MINE)

The Greek word for *remain* in this passage is *meno,* which means "to stay (in a given place, state, relation or expectancy)."[3] Jesus wants us to have the fruit of faith that is always expecting great things. *Meno* is connected to words such as "abide, continue, dwell, endure, be present, remain, stand, tarry." In other words, we must abide, remain, continue and dwell with the Lord in order to bear fruit that will last. Jesus was saying that He wants us to remain in Him so that we can conceive and bear fruit that will remain—to become spiritually pregnant while at the same time negating the plans of the Accuser. How can one get pregnant if one never stops long enough to be intimate before running off to another place? We must *remain.*

When we remain in Christ, we cannot hear the whispers of the devil. When we are properly positioned and are close enough to the Lord to hear His whisper, then we are able to be impregnated with His seed concerning our future. This is exactly what Elijah did after he heard God's whisper: He developed fruit that remained—in Elisha. Dear ones, our triumph depends upon our being properly positioned for conception and reproduction.

Will you *abide* in Him? *Continue* with Him? *Dwell* with Him?

> Every branch in me that beareth not fruit he taketh away; and every branch that beareth fruit, he purgeth it, that it may bring forth more fruit. Now ye are clean through the word which I have spoken unto you. *Abide* in me, and I in you. As the branch cannot bear fruit of itself, except it *abide* in the vine; no more can ye, except ye *abide* in me. I am the vine, ye are the branches: He that *abideth* in me, and I in him, the same bringeth forth much fruit: for without me ye can do nothing. If a man *abide* not in me, he is cast forth as a branch, and is withered; and men gather them, and cast them into the fire, and they are burned. If ye *abide* in me, and my words *abide* in you, ye shall ask what ye will, and it shall be done unto you. Herein is my Father glorified, *that ye bear much fruit;* so shall ye be my disciples.
>
> —JOHN 15:2–8, KJV (EMPHASIS MINE)

The only way we can bear fruit that gives God glory is to abide in Him. *Abiding* means to "live in Christ," "remain with Christ" and "dwell in Christ." When we *abide* in Him we are permanently attached to Him. How could we not pay attention in an environment like that? We need to become so attached to Jesus that we begin to think as He does, act as He does, love as He does and trust the Father as He does. When we pay attention to His Word, we learn to trust our heavenly Father as Jesus did. We will say and do only what the Father says. We will see what Jesus saw. The fruit that "remains" is fruit that has been birthed only through relationship—being properly positioned—with Christ.

2. **In order to position ourselves properly we must also remember that Satan wants to engage us in a battle of the mind. Unless we meditate on the Lord and His Word, we make ourselves vulnerable to the violent whispers of the enemy.**

> Blessed [happy, fortunate, prosperous, and enviable] is the man who walks and lives not in the counsel of the ungodly [following their advice, their plans and purposes], nor stands [submissive and inactive] in the path where sinners walk, nor sits down [to relax and rest] where the scornful [and the mockers] gather. But his delight and desire are in the law of the Lord, and on His law (the precepts, the instructions, the teachings of God) he habitually *meditates* (ponders and studies) by day and by night.
>
> —PSALM 1:1–2, AMP (EMPHASIS MINE)

If we delight in the precepts and teachings of God and continually meditate on His Word, then we will be happy and prosperous. The translation *prosperous* in this passage is not simply referring to money but to a state of growth, maturity and progress that later bears fruit. It is important, therefore, to walk in godly counsel and meditate on His Word in order to be prosperous in God. Furthermore, when we meditate on His Word, we are also meditating on Jesus, for Jesus is the Word.

Vine's Expository Dictionary of Biblical Words defines *meditate* as "to attend to . . . , practice. . . . , be diligent."[4] The word *attend* is the root of the word *attention*. Sometimes meditating means simply to pay attention to what God is saying. And each time we read the

Bible, we need to gain new reverence for His Word, paying close attention to how He speaks through it.

When I was a child I was hyperactive; always moving, creating and doing. My parents would attempt to give me clear instructions, but I kept moving and dashing around, not paying much attention to them. One of them would then stop me by saying, "Halt. Sandie, look at me. Watch my mouth. Pay attention to what I am saying." In the same way, we must allow God to slow us down and give Him our full attention, so that we can clearly hear the words He desires to speak to us.

Many things distract us from paying *attention* to God and His Word, the biggest of which is the whisper of Satan. Dear ones, unless we purposefully pay close attention to God's Word and heed His direction, the enemy will imprison us to our past.

I am so determined for destiny that I will set my face like flint toward my future. Will you join me in a greater pursuit of completeness and fullness that can come only by *abiding in* and *meditating on* the Living Word?

LISTEN TO THE WHISPERS OF THE LORD

Dear reader, take heed: The words of the Accuser are attached to a curse of death. He will falsely accuse you, lie to you and say that your victories in God do not matter; he will try to persuade you to run in the opposite direction of your future and then turn you away from God. The Accuser will frustrate, intimidate, violate and infiltrate every entrance allowed. Do not open the door to the enemy. Do not allow him to whisper into your ear. I cannot emphasize this enough: If you can hear him, then he is too close. And if he does get close enough that you can whisper, then you must recognize his voice as opposite of what God says and shut the door.

Take a moment right now and ask the Lord to empower you

to wait on Him and hear His whispers so that you can conceive your future. The Lord has reproduction planned for you. God has increase, breakthrough, anointing, ministry opportunities and deliverance planned for your future. Listen for His whisper. I encourage you to pray this simple prayer:

> *Lord, empower me to _____ (your words here) so that I cannot only bear fruit but also have fruit that remains. I desire to hear Your still, small voice. Whisper to me, and empower me to fulfill my destiny—the destiny You have planned for me. In Jesus' name, Amen.*

Now allow me to pray for you:

> *Father, I ask that You lead each person reading this book on the path that brings completeness and fruitfulness. I pray that You make Your face shine upon them so that they may be delivered from the past (see Psalm 80:7). I ask that You visit them and answer them with Your awesome deeds of righteousness and that You renew a steadfast spirit within them. I thank You for the assurance they have in Christ and that You have promised to never cast them from Your presence or remove Your Holy Spirit from them (see Psalm 51:10–12).*
>
> *Forgive all of us for not abiding in You and for the times we have not paid attention to Your leadings and promptings. Help us to trust You—to believe You for everything. Thank You for continuing to transform us into Your likeness.*
>
> *[Add any of your own words. . . .]*
> *In the mighty name of Jesus, I pray, Amen.*

5

Lie #4:
LET ME BUILD MY FORTRESS IN YOUR MIND

For though we walk in the flesh, we do not war after the flesh:
(For the weapons of our warfare are not carnal, but mighty
through God to the pulling down of strong holds.)

2 CORINTHIANS 10:3–4, KJV

One of the fiercest battles we fight against evil occurs on the battle-field of the mind. Satan, the Accuser, desires to possess a person's mind and establish a fortress around it—*his* fortress. Dear ones, it is the intent of the Accuser to build a fortress in our minds in order to "lock out" the voice of God's Spirit.

Our enemy begins by falsely accusing God. He will first speak lies to us, hoping we will listen and accept those lies as truth. If the Accuser can convince us that God is not trustworthy and if we continue to listen to false accusations concerning God's faithfulness, then our thoughts will be poisoned with doubt and unbelief. If he is able to convince us that God is not really able to care for us, protect us and perfect us, then he can move right in and begin to build his fortress. This is the goal of the Accuser: to cause us to doubt God and His Word. A lack of faith in God's unconditional love will cause our hearts to turn from God, therefore opening the door of our hearts to more evil seductions from our enemy.

Once Satan has seduced us to believe the lies about God, he begins to hurl other false accusations against us to see if we will swallow those lies as well. He falsely accuses us and lies to us concerning ourselves and our destiny. Each lie he speaks builds another wall. Lie after lie builds a fortress, and over time our minds become almost impregnable. Our Accuser has then established a well-fortified area within our belief systems that becomes a satanic fortress in our minds and robs us of any potential to develop the mind of Christ. Finally, he wages battle against us to protect his evil fortress whenever we attempt to renew our minds and renounce his lies.

But, dear ones, we have hope. God promises to give us the keys to breakthrough so that we can break free from the lies of our Accuser.

THE BATTLE FOR THE MIND

Most of us are fully aware that when we refer to the mind we are usually referring to a higher function of the brain. I am not a neurologist and certainly cannot explain the biological and neurological functions of our human brain. Yet I know we all can agree that the mind is much more than just a part of the body.

As we search for deeper understanding concerning the mind,

we must study the original Hebrew and Greek. The Hebrew word most often used for *mind* is *nephesh,* which refers to a person and his/her life.[1] Interestingly, it also refers to a person's soul, appetite and, of course, mind. The Greek word for *mind, phroneo,* means "to set one's mind on a thing."[2]

Dear believer, on what is your mind set? You are in a battle for your mind, and Satan wants to imprison your mind within his fortress. Satan knows that if he can persuade you to set your mind on his accusations, then he can imprison you. He will seduce you, capture you, steal your belief system concerning truth, and take you hostage in the fortress he has built around your mind.

THE FORTRESSES OF OUR MINDS

The Greek word for fortress, *ouhutoma,* is also the same Greek word used to describe a prison.[3] Think about what a fortress is, how it is shaped and how it protects what is inside. It is an almost impregnable wall that keeps enemies out but also guards the things within. It is the same with the fortresses of our minds.

Satan's accusatory but persuasive words are usually what he uses to gain entrance into our minds. These words later become strongholds, or fortresses. Paul refers to these strongholds in 2 Corinthians 10:4. They are the lies that the devil, the Accuser, has ingrained into our minds and belief systems. They result in negative thoughts and a sense of powerlessness that the enemy uses to exert power over us. He knows that if he can speak his lies and we keep receiving them, then he has the solid foundation for his fortress. These fortresses built of lies keep negative thoughts protected within that citadel but also guard that citadel from any intrusion of God's Word.

Have you ever wondered why you feel imprisoned and not

able to experience total freedom in Christ? Believers, unfortunately Satan has built prison cells in our minds and locked us in a cell. He desires a lofty position in our thought lives; he is seeking to establish a "seated position," or a "seat of Satan," in our minds.

We all want to believe God, but when we cannot do so, it is time to examine the walls of our minds and search for prison bars.

SATAN WILL PROTECT HIS FORTRESS

Have you ever experienced times when your enemy digs up your past and presents it to you time and time again to drown you in shame, hopelessness and despair? If you have doubted God and His Word or even doubted your own ability to follow God and become transformed into His divine image, then Satan has built a stronghold in your belief system. If your Accuser has done this—and I do not know of anyone who has not had this happen sometime in his or her lifetime—then he is attempting to build a demonic stronghold (a fortress) in your mind. And he will do whatever he can to protect it.

Several years ago while on a ministry trip, I visited England. One of my "dreams come true" was to visit a castle. As I approached the castle set high upon a hill, its solid, towering walls of stone seemed literally to stretch into heaven. Once I was inside the castle, I could see for miles around; the surrounding view of the countryside was magnificent. The castle obviously had been built in a strategic location, for an approaching enemy could have been spotted from many miles away and its high position would have made it almost impenetrable. Though enemies had warred to capture this stronghold, the fortress had frustrated many plans of its opposition. I pondered the frustration of kings and armies who had tried to "take the stronghold" and failed.

I realized that the fortress of my mind was quite similar to this medieval castle. During fierce battles against my Accuser, I would usually blame myself or revert to shame, insecurity and inferiority. For years I had tried to control my thoughts, only to realize I was actually contending with an evil fortress, a demonic stronghold.

The word *stronghold* comes from the Greek word *ochuroma*.[4] This is one of the oldest words in the New Testament and was originally used to describe a type of castle or a fortress. The purpose of a fortress was to intimidate intruders from scaling its monstrous walls or from breaking inside. Keeping intruders outside was the goal.

When the Accuser builds a fortress in the mind, he also goes to great lengths to protect what he has mastered. He desires to guard his strongholds in our lives. As much as I have written over the years on spiritual strongholds, it was a new revelation to me to see that Satan works diligently to defend what he has built.

Indeed, Satan is an evil prince of darkness who attempts to guard the false belief system he has built in our minds. He is good at protecting what he has built and will use all his power to protect it. He is a master of disguise and will deliberately attempt to reinvent himself. Though he takes on many different names and functions, he is still the devil—cunning, crafty and often subtle.

THE AMORITE SPIRIT

A *mafia* is a form of organized crime, and Satan's cohorts are like a demonic mafia, for our Accuser is organized with his demonic structuring. Ephesians 6:12 (KJV) describes the different levels of Satan's kingdom of darkness:

> For we wrestle not against flesh and blood, but against
> principalities, against powers, against the rulers of the dark-
> ness of this world, against spiritual wickedness in high
> places.

This Scripture proves that the kingdom of darkness has principalities, powers and rulers that have established themselves in
"high places." In spiritual warfare, our goal is to expose Satan's
plans to remain in an exalted position in our lives and then to
tear him down.

One spirit that has teamed up with the Accuser and works
alongside him to battle against and accuse God's people is the
Amorite spirit. The name *Amorite* means "a sayer."[5] *Strong's* translates *Amorite* similarly, but adds "a sense of publicity and prominence" to the one doing the talking.[6] When this spirit speaks—or
falsely accuses—it therefore is seeking a prominent position in our
lives (a "high place"), and it has mastered its ability to persuade
us to listen.

Fausset's Bible Dictionary defines the *Amorite* as "the dweller on
the summits,"[7] and *Strong's* also describes an Amorite as a "mountaineer."[8] In biblical times, those who dwelled in the mountains
were considered to be the most warlike, so any army that came up
against the Amorites knew they had better be prepared for a fight.
In the same way today, the Amorite spirit will go toe-to-toe to
keep its ground—or its high place (mountain). The Accuser and
his cohorts enjoy being able to speak over a person's life and will
fight to remain a familiar voice.

When we are determined to "go higher" in God, the enemy
fights any forward movement. And since the Amorite is a "sayer,"
it establishes itself in the high places and attempts to fight with
words of intimidation, shouting false accusations from the "moun-
taintops." Often this strategy works: The enemy merely hurls false

accusations and words of intimidation, and we back off. In such instances, the enemy has won without even sharpening one single sword. The Amorite then attempts to build a fortress upon its ability to deceive and lie to us.

King David was confronted with the voice of an Amorite-fueled spirit that had teamed up with the Jebusites. In his battle for Jebus, as David and his army began to take the higher ground, the Jebusites hurled intimidating accusations against him with a "mountaineer voice" that was determined to keep its ground. The Jebusites shouted false accusations such as, "David, even the blind and lame could defeat you!" Now that's a demonic sayer, isn't it? The Jebusites were operating under the same demonic influence as the Amorites. David, however, chose to seize the fortress rather than retreat. Then he required the Israelites to exterminate completely the entire Amorite army. What a wonderful biblical example of going up and defeating a fortress of the enemy for God.

Does that mountaineer spirit, the Amorite, dwell on your mountain? Is the devil attempting to keep the ground that belongs to you? As you attempt to go higher in God, does the enemy shout to you with a voice of intimidation, "Go back—you are too weak and helpless to take this ground"? If you have been called to rule and reign with Christ, as I know you have, then you must be like David and be determined to take the high places.

Dear ones, it is high time (pun intended) that we realize we are to take the high places and tear down every false voice that has attempted to occupy the land in which we belong. Yes, we are the ones who are destined to "go up" and "tear down" altars of wickedness as we rule and reign in Christ. As King David took the higher ground at Jebus, we have the same destiny. Let's get busy and put the enemy underfoot.

THE FIVE AMORITE KINGS

As we seek to learn more about the Amorite spirit, it is helpful to examine the accusing voices of the five Amorite kings who opposed Joshua in Canaan. These kings will help us to develop a targeted strategy to discern the lies of the Amorite spirit and become empowered to defeat it, thus tearing down the fortress that our Accuser has built in our minds.

The five kings of the Amorites, who lived in the mountains (the high places), joined forces against the Gibeonites. The Gibeonites then sent a plea for help to Joshua at the Gilgal campsite:

> And the men of Gibeon sent unto Joshua to the camp to Gilgal, saying, Slack not thy hand from thy servants; come up to us quickly, and save us, and help us: for all the kings of the Amorites that dwell in the *mountains* are gathered together against us.
>
> —JOSHUA 10:6, KJV (EMPHASIS MINE)

Upon receiving the cry for help to "come quickly" and "save" them, Joshua marched all night with his entire army, including his most skilled warriors, and took the enemy by surprise. Israel knew it had to tear down idols in the high places and claim those places for the Lord, so Israel was committed to possessing the higher ground. The enemy, however, was determined to keep its territory and would not give it up without a fight.

Notice that the Gibeonites asked Joshua to "come quickly" and "save us." An element of panic is involved here. Beloved, the words from your Accuser are so devastating that you need immediate rescue. The way to be rescued is to speak God's Word. God says that as soon as the Amorite speaks to you, submit to the Lord, rebuke the enemy, and he will flee. This proves the power of

Satan's accusations and "sayings," as well as how his lies intimidate us to back off and fear him. But it also proves that God's Word is more powerful; we therefore have nothing to fear as long as we stay rooted in Him.

Now let's take a closer look at the names and accompanying "accusing" voices of the five Amorite kings.

1. King Adoni-zedek of Jerusalem

Strong's states that *Adoni-zedek* is a Hebrew name that means "lord of justice." The name is derived from a root word referring to a "controller" or "sovereign master."[9]

Isn't it interesting that a fortress or stronghold always has a sovereign king or ruler? The Amorite "sayer," who attempts to be master over you, will speak of his ability to control you. He will put fear in your heart, and you will end up feeling so out of control that *you* actually revert to being controlling and manipulating. Many times, when this spirit is active, we automatically respond in ways that try to control God and control our own future. We make decisions without praying and seeking godly direction and counsel.

Strong's also links this king's name with the word *tsedeq,* which refers to "prosperity."[10] I am convinced that during seasons when prosperity is challenged, the "sayer" spirit rises up to speak lies concerning God's faithfulness to provide for His children. This opens the door wide to the spirit of Mammon. I have committed an entire book to this subject. You will want to read my book *Crushing the Spirits of Greed and Poverty*[11] to empower you to cycle out of doubt and unbelief concerning God's desire to provide during such uncertain times.

Beloved, we must be on guard when our breakthroughs are being opposed by our enemy. Satan seeks to punish God by causing us to believe his lies over God's promises. As we battle the

Amorite spirit, we must be on the lookout for the ways in which Satan tries to "lord" over us and control us. We must also listen to God's Word regarding our prosperity and renounce what the Accuser tries to tell us.

2. Hoham of Hebron

The name *Hoham* means "a multitude; a great multitude; Jehovah protects the multitude (root: to make a noise; the motion of people; to destroy). He crushed."[12] This name identifies our enemy as a vast army, or a multitude, of Satan that targets God's people with destruction.

When the Amorites attacked Gibeon, they moved forward in "troops," or large numbers:

> Then the five kings of the Amorites—the kings of Jerusalem, Hebron, Jarmuth, Lachish and Eglon—joined forces. They moved up with all their troops and took up positions against Gibeon and attacked it.
>
> —JOSHUA 10:5

This name also talks about making a noise and coming to destroy. Scripture says that the enemy comes to kill, steal and destroy, and one of his tactics is to make a loud sound as he comes. This noise is the voice of the Accuser, who likes to "sound off." Satan desires to crush us with his words. The old saying goes, "Sticks and stones may break my bones, but words will never hurt me." This statement is so untrue; words do hurt, and Satan knows that. He uses his words, as well as the false accusations of others, and then he seduces us to believe them. As a result, he builds a fortress around those words. The negative words become locked in our memory banks, like a computer chip that downloads during adversity.

Yet we can remain steadfast and hope in God. We can choose to take our rightful position as overcomers in Christ, empowered to be in His army so that we run through the enemy's troops and leap over walls (see 2 Samuel 22:30). In other words, God gives us hinds' feet for high places. We are destined to take the higher ground. We will run past Satan's fortified areas and leap over the castle walls and take back our minds. Rise up now and declare: *I have the mind of Christ.*

3. Piram of Jarmuth

Piram is a Hebrew name that means "wildly." In a secondary sense, it refers to the name as "one running wild, as a wild donkey or an onager."[13]

Have you ever received a phone call from your doctor's office asking you to commit to a follow-up appointment? Instantly, your mind begins to run wild with negative thoughts. This is a prime example of how the "sayer" spirit operates. He says, "You have cancer," and immediately you are wondering if you will have to undergo chemotherapy, or if you will even live long enough to have treatment—and you do not even know yet if you are sick.

The enemy runs wild in our thoughts sometimes, doesn't he? Dear ones, we must take our wild thoughts captive and cause them to surrender to God's perfect will concerning our futures. When our imaginations run riotously, we also will run wild in every direction. When a negative report flies through our mental neighborhoods, we must be smart and prepare for the storm. It is time to batten down the hatches, lock the doors, get out the Word, take every thought captive to the obedience of Christ—and *stand.*

The name of this king also is connected to another root word that means "bearing fruit." In the previous chapter I discussed our need to bear fruit. It is important to remember that we cannot truly bear fruit if we keep listening to the abortive lies of the enemy.

4. Japhia of Lachish

Japhia refers to a "light," and since we are discussing the Amorite demonic "sayer," I believe this name represents a false light and a false voice. This is where a spirit of deception gains entrance.

Strong's uses the word *yapha* as Japhia's root origin, and *yapha* means "to shine, be light, shew self, (cause to) shine (forth)."[14] This word reminds me of the way the enemy attempts to show off his powers in a prideful way.

Don't you just hate the devil? He is sneaky and fights dirty. Have you ever seen someone who "fights dirty," who hits "below the belt"? Such a person fights in ways that cross the line. If we are not on our guard, then Satan can attack us by fighting dirty. I am infuriated every time I am not on my guard and I allow the Accuser's lies to shine brighter than God's Word, or Christ in me.

Being on guard means allowing the glory of God to shine brighter than the "light" of the Accuser. In order to battle a spirit like the Amorite, which is a spirit of deception, we must show forth more of Jesus. The more of Jesus we have inside our hearts and the more we are transformed into His divine image, the more of the devil's lights we can punch out.

Care to join me? Begin to declare with me that you will arise and shine for His glory.

5. Debir of Eglon

Debir is a name of Hebrew origin that refers to one who is an "oracle." *Strong's* connects the name to a root word, *dabar,* which also denotes oracle manifestations, as "to speak, to answer, to appoint, and (through oracle demonstration) to lead and command." This name implies the opportunity to "subdue" through speech.[15] Once more we are reminded of the power of Satan's words.

Think about this for a minute: An Amorite spirit has the ability to subdue us if we listen to its words. The Accuser sets out to point (appoint) our lives in the wrong direction, speak lies concerning us, demean us and our significance, and negate God's power with words of doubt and unbelief. Our sure retaliation is to proclaim what God says. This will ensure our victory over the Accuser. Again, if we speak His Word, then we have a quick "rescue."

The name of this king reminds me of the Oracle of Delphi. Delphi was a sanctuary dedicated to the Greek god Apollo that exerted considerable influence throughout the Greek world. Its origins were rooted in Greek mythology. According to the myth, a huge serpent named Pytho had an oracle on Mount Parnassus and was famous for predicting events. Apollo slew this serpent, and Apollo subsequently was called Pythius. It was believed that everyone who "predicted" future events was influenced by the spirit of Apollo Pythius.[16] For many years, the Oracle was consulted for all major undertakings—wars, the founding of colonies, and so forth. Apollo supposedly spoke through this oracle, which has an obvious connection with the same evil spirit that was behind the Amorite king named Debir of Eglon.

Priestesses of the Oracle of Delphi were called *pythia,* a derivative of *python,* the Greek word for *divination.* We all know what a python does, don't we? It squeezes the life out of its victims. In the same way, the spirit of the Accuser works closely with a spirit of divination to falsely prophesy to us and steal our life in Christ.

The enemy desires a voice in our lives. He wants to falsely prophesy concerning our future. Beloved, if we listen to the false prophecies of our enemy, he will squeeze the life right out of us. We must remain on guard against the words and oracles of the Accuser.

JOSHUA'S VICTORY

Let's look with a little more depth at Joshua's response to the Amorites. Upon receiving the Gibeonites' panicked plea for help, Joshua marched up from Gilgal with his entire army. The Lord told Joshua, "Do not be afraid of them; I have given them into your hand. Not one of them will be able to withstand you" (Joshua 10:8). Let's look at what followed:

> After an all-night march from Gilgal, Joshua took [the Amorites] by surprise. The LORD threw them into confusion before Israel, who defeated them in a great victory at Gibeon. Israel pursued them along the road going up to Beth Horon and cut them down all the way to Azekah and Makkedah. As they fled before Israel on the road down from Beth Horon to Azekah, the LORD hurled large hailstones down on them from the sky, and more of them died from the hailstones than were killed by the swords of the Israelites.
>
> —JOSHUA 10:9–11

It is important to notice several points about Joshua's response. First, Joshua marched with his entire army, including the best of his fighting men (see verse 7). If you are in a battle against this "trash-talking" spirit, then consider this: You are chosen as God's best to be in this battle. I know Satan has probably falsely accused you and said that you are weak and unfit, but the devil is a liar, and what he says is never true. You must be the one in charge of what is declared. Let me be bold here and tell you that it is time for you to shout out against your Accuser. Say to your Accuser now, "Devil, the Lord rebuke you. I am God's chosen, well equipped for battle. God has promised me victory."

Second, God told Joshua not to be afraid. The Accuser has been lying to you and telling you that you are a coward because you are experiencing fear. Let me assure you that fear is a normal response to battle. God encourages us not to fear, fully realizing that it is a force with which to contend and that He will empower us with courage. We must always remember that courage is not having the absence of the feeling of fear; rather, courage empowers us to press beyond the present danger. God is saying to you, "Fear not. Have courage. I have already gone before you and defeated your enemies." And, just as He promised Joshua, "Not one of them will be able to withstand you."

Third, Joshua took the enemy by surprise. Though it was an all-night march for Israel, they caught the enemy off guard. Dear believer, you may have been in the same battle for years, but God is about to perform a surprise attack for you. Suddenly and by surprise, He will defeat the Accuser on your behalf. Do not ever quit believing that.

Fourth, the Lord knows how to fight your battles for you. In this case, God hurled confusion into the camp of the enemy. I love it when God takes what I battle (confusion) and puts it back on the enemy. We can trust Him to have the best battle strategy.

Fifth, we need to be willing to pursue our enemy. To *pursue* means to chase down. *Strong's* notes the Hebrew word *radaph,* which is a root word meaning "to run after (usually with a hostile intent)."[17] This means Joshua and his army chased their enemies in order to persecute them for even thinking they could attack God's chosen.

Joshua and his army did not stop at victory. They pursued the enemy. And Joshua was so determined to find his enemy and destroy him that he led Israel in cutting him down: "Israel pursued [the Amorites] along the road going up to Beth Horon and *cut them down* all the way to Azekah and Makkedah" (Joshua 10:10, emphasis mine). Yes, the sword was used in every possible way.

In the same way today, we do not celebrate a victory just because the enemy grabs his goods and flees. What is the use of going to war if we are only going to settle for a victory? No, we can no longer tolerate our enemy, and we must cut him down completely. We must cut off his head as David did Goliath. And we must cut him down in order to capture the spoils of war, right? We want the spoils because God promises them to us.

How dare the devil attack *you*! Who does he think he is, anyway? He thinks he is the chief operating officer over your life, but this is God's position. It is time to rise up and pursue your Accuser. Do not stop at victory. Cut him down completely.

ISRAEL PURSUED ITS ENEMIES TO TWO CITIES

Note in Joshua 10:10 that Israel pursued its enemies all the way to Azekah and Makkedah. The Amplified Bible says:

> And the Lord caused [the enemies] to panic before Israel, who slew them with a great slaughter at Gibeon, and chased them along the way that goes up to Beth-horon, and smote them as far as Azekah and Makkedah.
>
> —Joshua 10:10, AMP

In order to pinpoint our road to victory, it is important to look closely at both of these biblical places.

Azekah

Azekah is a Hebrew name that means "to grub over."[18] There is not much I detest more than grub worms eating away at my St.

Augustine grass. They eat underground, attacking the root systems during the winter. When I am expecting my yard to be green when spring arrives, I am disappointed to see nothing but brown. When you plant a yard of St. Augustine grass and the lawn develops huge brown dead patches, you can be sure the grub worms have been at work, colonizing in your territory.

Similarly, if we are not alert, then the enemy will eat away at our godly root systems and destroy our future. He wants to cut off our future expectations, our destinies in Christ, from the roots. Do you often sow godly seeds and believe for breakthrough and fruitfulness, only to find that grubby devil eating away at the root of your breakthrough and blessing?

Azekah also means "maggot" and "scarlet."[19] Ugh, need I go further? *Strong's* connects these two meanings with a further definition: "the dye made from the dried body of the female worm called 'coccus ilicus.' "[20]

Dear ones, the Accuser seeks to eat away at our godly root systems. Yet Jesus' shed blood on the cross destroys every "worm" that seeks to do so. Furthermore, Rahab hung a scarlet thread from her window as a sign to Joshua that it was safe to enter Jericho. That scarlet thread was a sure sign of victory, and its scarlet color came from a dye made from the dried body of a female worm. Dear believer, God can use even a maggot or a grub worm to accomplish His divine purposes.

Joshua cut down his enemies at the "grub worm" stage. Today, the Lord Jesus desires to restore every place in your life that appears to be eaten away. Yes, God will restore what the worms have eaten away in your life.

> And I will restore to you the years that the locust
> hath eaten, the cankerworm, and the caterpillar, and the

palmerworm, my great army which I sent among you. And ye shall eat in plenty, and be satisfied, and praise the name of the LORD your God, that hath dealt wondrously with you: and my people shall never be ashamed.

—JOEL 2:25–26, KJV

Let's look at one final point regarding the city of Azekah. *Strong's* says that Azekah was a city "fenced about."[21] It was a safe haven. Believer, God has placed a fence around us. He is our God and has provided protection, care, deliverance and a fortress around us. After all, He says He is our strong high tower and our fortress. But God did even more for Joshua:

As [the Amorites] fled before Israel on the road down from Beth Horon to Azekah, the LORD hurled large hailstones down on them from the sky, and more of them died from the hailstones than were killed by the swords of the Israelites. . . . So the sun stood still, and the moon stopped, till the nation avenged itself on its enemies. . . . The sun stopped in the middle of the sky and delayed going down about a full day. There has never been a day like it before or since, a day when the LORD listened to a man. Surely the LORD was fighting for Israel! Then Joshua returned with all Israel to the camp at Gilgal.

—JOSHUA 10:11, 13–15

Dear ones, just as He did with Joshua, the Lord will hurl huge hailstones down on your enemies when you pursue them. He will even stop time, as He did for Joshua, and let you battle in the light so that you are guaranteed victory.

Makkedah

Joshua pursued and cut down the army of the five kings, but the five kings themselves fled and were hiding in the cave at Makkedah. Let's take a closer look at what happened:

Now the five kings had fled and hidden in the cave at *Makkedah.* When Joshua was told that the five kings had been found hiding in the cave at *Makkedah,* he said, "Roll large rocks up to the *mouth* of the cave, and post some men there to guard it. But don't stop! Pursue your enemies, attack them from the rear and don't let them reach their cities, for the LORD your God has given them into your hand."

So Joshua and the Israelites *destroyed them completely*— almost to a man—but *the few who were left reached their fortified cities.* The whole army then returned safely to Joshua in the camp at *Makkedah, and no one uttered a word* against the Israelites.

Joshua said, "*Open the mouth* of the cave and bring those five kings out to me." So they brought the five kings out of the cave—the kings of Jerusalem, Hebron, Jarmuth, Lachish and Eglon.

When they had brought these kings to Joshua, he summoned all the men of Israel and said to the army commanders who had come with him, "Come here and put your *feet on the necks of these kings.*" So they came forward and placed their feet on their necks.

Joshua said to them, "*Do not be afraid; do not be discouraged. Be strong and courageous.* This is what the LORD will do to all the enemies you are going to fight." Then Joshua struck and killed the kings and hung them on five trees, and they were left hanging on the trees until evening.

At sunset Joshua gave the order and they took them down from the trees and threw them into the cave where they had been hiding. At the mouth of the cave they placed large rocks, which are there to this day.

That day Joshua took Makkedah. He put the city and its king to the sword and totally destroyed everyone in it. He left no survivors. And he did to the king of Makkedah as he had done to the king of Jericho.

—JOSHUA 10:16–28 (EMPHASIS MINE)

Notice that some of the Amorite soldiers fled to their *fortified cities*. Believer, the enemy will always attempt to run back to his fortified place in your mind. Especially after deliverance, the enemy seeks an area in your mind and heart that is well fortified with shame, guilt, insecurity, condemnation, rejection, abandonment, etc.

In addition we ourselves often run to what is fortified, or familiar, even if it is bondage. An old fortress may appear at first to be safe and secure—because it is familiar. But we must begin to build our fortress upon what God says about us and not what Satan says. This is the only thing that will demolish an old fortress and empower His fortress to be built. This fortress of His truth will be our new foundation. If we build upon that, then His truth—and His truth alone—will enable us to stand against our Accuser.

According to *Strong's*, *Makkedah* implies the name "shepherd."[22] Dear ones, this meaning is so important to us as children of the Most High God. God is our great Shepherd, and it is to Him we should run. He should be our fortress, or fortified and familiar place. Let us run to and seek refuge in Him, for it is there—and there only—that we can find true refuge and safety.

Indeed, the Lord Himself led the Amorites to the cave of *Makkedah*, for He had a plan all along to bless Israel. As Israel pressed forward into victory and the Amorites fled, "no one uttered a word against the Israelites" (Joshua 10:21). The enemy understood the determination of Israel and backed off of his accusations.

The devil knows when to back off and will do so when he is absolutely sure that we know who we are in Christ and that we have the upper hand. When we have truly overcome the stronghold he built in our minds, he will no longer accuse us. When we have achieved the victory, the devil cannot utter a word in our minds. This is when we know we have victory over the Accuser. Even if he does try to slip in and utter a noise, it will not take root because the fortress has been taken.

Dear ones, if we make up our minds to defeat the devil, then God will be faithful to empower us to pursue and overtake him. We must believe only what God says about us.

Isn't it interesting that Joshua commanded his soldiers to put a stone on the "mouth" of the cave? He kept them imprisoned inside until the Israelites had pursued their enemies all the way back to their cities and destroyed them completely. Then he brought out the five kings and hanged them. Afterward, he placed their bodies back in the cave and sealed the mouth of it with large rocks.

In the same way that Joshua sealed the "mouth" of his enemies, we must seal the mouth of our Accuser. We must put the "fortress" that the enemy has built in our minds and its "king," our Accuser, to the sword and completely destroy them both, leaving no survivors. When we do to our Accuser what Joshua did to the king of Makkedah and his people, we will achieve victory. Beloved, if we will remain steady, persistent and in pursuit of our destiny, God promises to close the mouth that speaks of shame, fear and past failures.

THE ACCUSER'S SPIRIT OF DECEPTION

I want to briefly look at the way the Accuser manifests as a spirit of deception, because this is one of the main ways he tries to build his fortress in our minds. I truly believe that if we examine closely this stronghold, then we will become empowered to overcome our enemy.

The dictionary defines *deception* as "being deceived," or "to be misled by a false appearance or statement" and "to be tricked."[23] The deception of the Accuser usually comes in the form of false prophecy, which is connected to "the angel of light," or Satan. False prophecy is not merely a person speaking an incorrect prophetic declaration. It also can be an evil spirit falsely prophesying into our futures, such as when the enemy declares, "You will never win this battle" or "You do not have the spiritual fortitude to take a strong stand. You will fail if you step out in faith."

Another trick of Satan is to lie concerning God. He will say, "God does not even know who you are. You are not important to God. If you step out in faith, then God will not honor your efforts."

Beloved, Satan will lie about us to others and will falsely accuse God to us. If we believe the lies, then we have become deceived. We must be on guard against the enemy falsely prophesying and speaking the opposite of what God says about us and our circumstances.

Furthermore, deception opens doors to many other spirits, such as doubt and unbelief, spirits of error, familiar spirits, legalism, slander and the occult. Most of these spirits are self-explanatory or I have already defined them in this book. I have been exposing the lies of the Accuser in almost every chapter.

Envision Satan opposing you. He reaches into his quiver for an arrow with which to strike you. He pulls out a particularly sharp arrow—one poisoned with enough venom to kill you. He places the arrow in his bow, aims and draws back. The tip of the arrow is aimed at your belief system. The Accuser wishes to poison your mind concerning your future and God's ability to empower you to overcome the wiles of our adversary. If you are not holding up your shield of faith when the arrow is released, then the venomous poison will infect every part of your being with the enemy's false accusations, slander and false prophecy. And if you do not immediately replace the lies with truth, then you are easily defeated.

HOW TO BATTLE THE STRONGHOLD

If you have ever tried to break out of your prison, you know how difficult the battle is. The minute we try to step out, we are attacked from all sides. This battle of the mind is real, and it is dark, ugly and demonic. It is spiritual warfare, and it is led by the prince of darkness.

If we, for example, reach out for deliverance through prayer ministry, the enemy fights to protect his fortress of lies. He will speak such words as:

- "You cannot trust them."
- "If you tell them what you are really like, then they will abandon you."
- "If anyone finds out your real struggles, then they will forsake you."
- "You will never be free. Do not even try. You have failed too many times."
- "It is hopeless. You are hopeless."

What words does the enemy use against you when you attempt to break free? Are you listening?

God's Word gives us several keys to battle the stronghold and break free from it. Let's take a look.

1. Set Your Mind on Things Above

First, Paul said, "Set your minds on things above, not on earthly things" (Colossians 3:2). When we set our minds on the things of God, we are not limiting our minds (souls, lives, reasoning, attitudes and ourselves) to the natural realm.

This explains the battle of the mind, doesn't it? The intent of the Holy Spirit is to teach us all truth concerning the impact that our minds have on our spirits and our futures. We must set our minds on the things above, so that we will have His supernatural insight.

2. Have the Mind of Christ

First Corinthians 2:16 states, "For who has known the mind of the Lord that he may instruct him? But we have the mind of Christ." Did you get that? We as believers have the mind of Christ. Our spiritual DNA empowers us to have the faith of God and think as He does. If we are created in His image, then He has also empowered us to have His mind, right? We are also given the divine ability to share His character, His attitudes, His creativity and His reasoning. Dear Ones, this was His gift to us at creation. The problem is that Satan has stolen it from us. It is now our job to take back our minds, and we must engage in spiritual warfare in order to do so.

When we have the mind of Christ, we have greater understanding. We then can think like Christ, live like Christ, develop a spirit like Christ, reason and create as Christ does and have a heart like Christ. Renewing the mind is the crux of spiritual warfare.

3. Do Not Fear Your Enemy

Paul refers to our ability to remain stable in our faith in God as we pull down strongholds: "For though we walk in the flesh, we do not war after the flesh: (For the weapons of our warfare are not carnal, but mighty through God to the pulling down of strong holds)" (2 Corinthians 10:3–4, KJV). We need not fear our enemy, for God will always overcome.

4. Take Every Thought Captive

Paul also encourages us to "demolish arguments and every pretension that sets itself up against the knowledge of God, and (to) take captive every thought to make it obedient to Christ" (2 Corinthians 10:5). To win the battle of the mind, we must deal with our wills and emotions.

5. Put His Word in Your Heart

The heart and mind are connected. Whatever is in your mind and heart, your mouth will confess. Since life and death are in the power of the tongue, it is clear that we must protect what is sown into our hearts and minds. Let me be blunt: If Satan has your heart, then he will also possess your mind.

You might wonder, "How in the world could the enemy possibly seize our hearts and minds and affect our confession, therefore causing us to disengage from fulfilling the promises of God?" Satan desires both the *heart* and the *mind* of God's children. Deuteronomy 30:14 says God's Word is "very near you, in your *mouth,* and in your *mind* and in your *heart,* so that you can *do* it" (AMP, emphasis mine). Notice the emphasis on the four words: *mouth, mind, heart* and *do.* What is this Scripture instructing us to *do?* We are to *do* what the "Word" says. The Hebrew word for *do* is *asah,* and in its broadest sense it means "to accomplish" and "to advance."[24] In order to advance and accomplish all that God desires for us, we must believe God's Word in our hearts and minds. And, conversely, if our hearts and minds are not bent on believing God's Word, then we will not be empowered to act upon the promises therein.

6. Speak God's Word, Not the Words of the Enemy

What is your attitude concerning yourself? What words do you speak over you and the situations you are facing? Are you engaged in pessimism, or are you speaking God's words of life?

Have you noticed that a pessimistic person is almost completely and predictably negative? A pastor could have a meeting, and if a pessimist is present he/she will oppose any step requiring faith.

Negativity attracts an Amorite spirit. If someone is negative, then the Amorite spirit can empower that person to "speak" negatively into the atmosphere, thus defiling all around. Satan seeks any opportunity to erect a death structure. Any meeting of two or more people where a spirit of pessimism is active kills any hope or faith in the room, and a death structure becomes a fortress.

God promises that we can be victorious, yet so many Christians are pessimistic. We need to speak God's Word, not the pessimistic words of our Accuser, over every situation, so that we can be empowered to tear down the fortress the enemy has erected.

CLOSING THE MOUTH OF THE ACCUSER

As we close this chapter, I encourage you to take a few moments to think about the ways in which the Accuser has been targeting you.

What words does the enemy use against you? Take a few moments and write them below.

I hear the enemy say to me these words every time I attempt to break free from his fortress:

Now let me ask you a few questions:

1. Have you stood your ground against the Accuser? Did you declare that you are the victor over his plans? If you have answered *yes,* then you have every right to stand your ground and believe that God, Himself, is closing the mouth of your enemy.

2. Can you now believe that the five strongholds (the five kings) of the Amorite spirit are completely silenced and destroyed?

3. If you have placed your faith in the last two challenges, then can you take one more step toward victory and believe that because of His blood, you have been set free from every undermining spirit (the grub worms of life) that attempts to usurp your authority in Christ?

I just know you answered yes to all the above. Now we will take one more step together down your freedom road. It is time to totally negate the sayings of the Accuser. Are you still with me in this? I sincerely pray so. You have pressed through so much to get to this intersection. Making a turn is necessary at this point, and I have such confidence in you.

It is time to use our weapons of warfare and oppose Satan's lies concerning us. If the Amorite stronghold has built a fortress in your mind, here's your chance to use the knowledge of this chapter as keys to open your prison doors. Jesus has already won the victory, but it is still up to you to break free. Take what you have learned and cast down the vain imaginations that the Accuser has spoken concerning you. Yes, he "imagines" your defeat; it is your responsibility to remove Satan from his exalted position.

Remember what Paul said:

> (For the weapons of our warfare are not carnal, but mighty through God to the pulling down of strong holds;) Casting down imaginations, and every high thing that exalteth itself against the knowledge of God, and bringing into captivity every thought to the obedience of Christ.

—2 CORINTHIANS 10:4–5, KJV

Look back for a moment at the words you have been hearing your Accuser speak to you. Now take some time and ask the Lord to give you a Scripture, a promise, that will negate what the enemy is declaring concerning your life. It will take some time, but you will be so glad that you did this. Remember to consider how the Amorite spirit attempts to hold us captive with its "sayings." Pay attention to the ways in which you have been deceived and defiled by the Accuser's false accusations, and then repent for believing the lies.

Once you have repented, stand up and give the Lord a shout of victory. Thank Him for His love and for sending Jesus to pay the ultimate price for your freedom. You have demolished the lies of the Accuser and are defeating the Amorite spirit. You are becoming more and more free.

Now allow me to pray for you:

> Lord, I thank You that You have given those reading this book powerful weapons to go to war and defeat the Accuser. As they cast down the imaginations that the Accuser uses to build his fortress in their minds and lock out the voice of God's Spirit, I am confident that You are defeating the enemy on their behalf. I pray that these believers will continue to take the sword of the Spirit, the Word of the Lord, and tear down the fortresses the Accuser has erected. I also pray that they will no longer suffer setbacks and misfortunes and that they will come into the full knowledge of who they are in Christ Jesus. Thank You, Lord, that You have promised to restore all that appears lost and that we can have hope for our future. I declare over these readers that they have the mind of Christ and that they will continue to remain focused on Your goodness and desire to see them walk in complete victory and freedom. In Jesus' name, Amen.

6

Lie #5:
WEAR MY GARMENTS

The Spirit of the Sovereign LORD is on me,
because the LORD has anointed me
to preach good news to the poor.
He has sent me to bind up the brokenhearted,
to proclaim freedom for the captives
and release from darkness for the prisoners . . .
to comfort all who mourn,
and provide for those who grieve in Zion—
to bestow on them . . . a garment of praise
instead of a spirit of despair.

ISAIAH 61:1–3

My past is one I wish I could change. My childhood was challenged with fears of rejection and perfectionism. I did not need the devil to beat up on me; I did enough beating up on myself.

In elementary school I was unattractive, skinny and short. When I began first grade, my hands were too small to hold a pencil, and I could not write well. My classmates made fun of me because my penmanship was so atrocious. My mother and dad worked with me every day after school to help me practice in my writing tablet, but it took an entire school year before I could master the feared lead pencil. I became so fearful of being ridiculed in class that when lunchtime came I would run home and hide in the closet. Each day that I was able to escape, the school principal would call home looking for me. Of course, my mother would be in a panic and called for a neighborhood search every time. I got smart and began to change hideouts, developing new skills in deception. I would hide in the neighbor's yard, different playhouses or tree houses. Once I even remained in the girls' restroom at school for the remainder of the day. I locked the restroom stall and stood on the toilet to remain hidden. I knew everyone was looking for me, but I did not care. The pain of rejection was too severe; the shame was too traumatic. The Accuser would bombard me with thoughts at night. I had tormenting dreams of being hauled in front of the class, my writing tablet displayed under a microscope. Even when no classmate was making fun of me, the Accuser was still talking. Eventually I learned to write properly, but the root of my problem was still there.

Isn't it amazing that the very thing of which I was accused and tormented—writing—is how the Lord uses me for His Kingdom now? Do you see how the Accuser targets our potential? I am living proof that he does.

Growing up, I also had extremely crooked teeth. I have a small mouth—not that you could tell by how much I love to talk—and it did not have enough space for my teeth. As a result, my teeth grew in twisted and deformed-looking. I refused to smile out of fear that my classmates would make fun of me once more. I wanted braces so badly. All of the "popular" girls in the sixth grade had them, and I wanted them, too. I begged, I pleaded—I just knew I would fit in better with the other girls if I had braces. I would grab a "Marks-a-lot" in my room at night, attempt to draw a straight line across my front teeth and dream of how beautiful I would be with a steel band that stretched across my entire mouth. I would smile big then and not fear rejection. Though it took several days for the black to wear off my teeth, I did not care. Well, I eventually got my braces, and they did make me look better, but again, the root of my problem did not go away.

You see, my problem was deeper than learning to write or needing braces. The problem in my life went much deeper than my height or my athletic ability. My problem was a deep sense of unworthiness that was continually fueled by the lies I believed—the lies of my Accuser.

The devil is such a liar. When we believe his lies, they then become perceived truths, and we act accordingly. The lie is still a lie, but if I buy in to the lie, it affects my life in disastrous ways. When I buy in to the lie, I am taking on the garment of shame.

Dear ones, the Accuser wants us to wear his garments, rather than the white garments of new life given to us by our Savior. The Accuser attempts to clothe us with the shame of our past, but the Lord wants us to experience His acceptance and divine love.

SHAME ASSESSMENT

What about you? Whose garments are you wearing?

As a small child, did you regularly experience your parents' praise? When you took your first step, did they applaud and cheer? When you ate the unappealing pureed spinach from the spoon in your mother's hand as she made airplane sounds and waved the spoon in swirling motions in the air, did she laugh with you and praise you with a "Good girl" or "Good boy"? Do you remember your parents regularly taking you in their arms, hugging you and praising you? Or were your parents the kind who withheld such affection and praise from you? Were they perhaps even abusive? Maybe you were too young then to remember whether or not your mother and father treated you as "good" or "acceptable," yet these early years can have quite an effect on the garments we wear, as they set the tone for everything that comes after.

What about your elementary school years? Do you recall a particularly smiling and encouraging teacher? Did your classmates accept you—no matter how tall you were, what clothes you wore, whether you wore glasses, how intelligent you were or how you performed in sports at recess? Or were these years traumatic ones? Were you continually rejected by your classmates? Did you have an absent parent who was never around? Did you feel as if you never fit in—anywhere? You probably remember these years with more detail.

What about your teenage years? Is high school a happy, idyllic memory for you? Did you have many friends and participate in a wealth of enjoyable activities? Did you perform well in academics? Or were these tremulous years when you felt as if you never fit in? Do you look back on them with painful memories? During these extremely formative years, it is even more important to be acceptable, wear designer clothing, have fashionable hairstyles and be on the "A" string in sports rather than a benchwarmer. These teenage years are usually our most impressionable—and certainly the most memorable. These years build onto the foundation already established in childhood and have a significant bearing on what garments we carry and wear into our adulthood.

What about now? In your adult years, you face even more challenges. Your jobs are performance-based, your relationships become even more intricate and challenging, your responsibilities multiply exponentially, you have the great joy and burden of serving as a good parent yourself—the list goes on and on. In your life now, what garments do you wear?

Are the recollections of your life filled with praise, acceptance, success and fulfillment? Or have you experienced abuse, rejection, abandonment, trauma and emotional pain? And who do you blame? When you think back on various periods of your life, do you blame yourself for bad decisions? Do you recall not using sound judgment and now blame yourself? Do you blame others for beating you down, abusing you to the point where you felt you had no worth? Are you unable to shake the pain and shame of your past?

Let's determine if you are dealing with a thread of shame, so that the Lord can heal you and give you a garment change. Place a check beside each ungodly belief with which you relate:

- ☐ I am unlovable.
- ☐ I am a bad person.
- ☐ I am a shameful person.
- ☐ I am to blame for my past.
- ☐ Everything is my fault.
- ☐ I can never do anything right.
- ☐ I can never do enough to please people.
- ☐ I dislike myself.
- ☐ I hate myself.
- ☐ I am a disappointment to everyone.
- ☐ I cannot please God no matter how hard I try.
- ☐ I am a victim.
- ☐ I must have done something wrong because I was abused.
- ☐ If I am not perfect, then I will remain unacceptable.
- ☐ I am fearful of making mistakes.

☐ I am a people-pleaser.

☐ I have to remain in control at all times.

☐ I am always misunderstood.

☐ I am ugly.

☐ I am unsuccessful and cannot do enough to be accepted.

Now count how many checks you have. If you have only one area checked, then you have a root of shame that Jesus wishes to heal. Dear believer, just one of these ungodly beliefs will enshroud you with depression and hopelessness, but if you checked more than five, then most likely you are tormented by the Accuser with thoughts of shame, failure and deep depression. Whether you checked just one or many, you have found the right book. Jesus desires to empower you to develop a renewed mind. Hang in there with me as we continue to gain revelation on the actions of the Accuser.

THE ACCUSER IS THE MAIN CULPRIT

The Accuser is fueled by your ungodly beliefs; in fact, *he* is one of the main culprits. Yes, he knows your weakness.

If there is pain in your past, then the Accuser will prey upon that pain. Fueled by your ungodly beliefs about yourself, your past, your abilities or lack thereof, your weaknesses, etc., the Accuser will pound you daily with negative thoughts concerning that pain and trauma. He will do everything he can to block your healing. And he also will falsely accuse God and say things to you such as:

- "God knew you were abused. He could have stopped it, but He does not care about you."

- "God does not love you as much as He loves other people."
- "God expects you to be perfect to please Him."
- "God hates sin. Because of your sin, you are unacceptable to Him."

Yes, the Accuser is behind all your ungodly beliefs in one way or another. He had a hand in your believing them in the first place, and he continually preys upon you to keep them alive and active.

Dear believer, the entire Bible is laced with heroes of faith who messed up. Yet God in His infinite mercy and love continued to forgive His people over and over—and over—again.

Yes, it is true that God hates sin, but He certainly does not hate *us*. He sent Jesus to be our Balm of Gilead, an anointed salve, to heal our wounds. Jesus went to the cross and shed His blood to cleanse us from sin.

BINDING UP THE BROKENHEARTED

Isaiah 61:1 speaks of how Jesus was sent with a purpose, and in Luke 4:18–19, Jesus declares His purpose by reading this very passage from Isaiah in the synagogue in His hometown of Nazareth:

> He went to Nazareth, where he had been brought up, and on the Sabbath day he went into the synagogue, as was his custom. And he stood up to read. The scroll of the prophet Isaiah was handed to him. Unrolling it, he found the place where it is written:
>
> "The Spirit of the Lord is on me,
> because he has anointed me

to preach good news to the poor.
He has sent me to proclaim freedom for the prisoners
and recovery of sight for the blind,
to release the oppressed,
to proclaim the year of the Lord's favor."

Then he rolled up the scroll, gave it back to the attendant
and sat down.
The eyes of everyone in the synagogue were fastened on
him, and he began by saying to them, "Today this scripture is
fulfilled in your hearing."

—LUKE 4:16–21

The original passage in Isaiah from which Jesus read that day in
the synagogue includes the following: "He has sent me to *bind up* the
brokenhearted, to proclaim freedom for the captives" (Isaiah 61:1,
emphasis mine). The Hebrew meaning for "bind up" is *chabash,* which
means "to wrap firmly (especially a turban, compress, or saddle)."
Strong's goes on to use words such as "(to) gird about, govern, heal
and wrap about."[1] The words "bind up," then, offer a picture of Jesus
covering our wounds with a huge Band-Aid. Jesus came, dear one,
to wrap up our bleeding wounds of shame and trauma. I do not
know the intimate details of your life, but we all have areas that need
healing and restoration. Jesus came to heal those. Shall we let Him?

What about the image of a tightly wrapped "turban" that also
is part of this definition? The turban is a large cloth still worn today
by many people in the Middle East that is wrapped many times
around the head. We already have discussed how Jesus desires to
renew our minds, and the turban gives us an image of Him "healing"
our heads. Indeed, He binds up and bandages all of the improper
thinking—mainly ungodly beliefs—that have hindered our destinies
and personal healing. I am so glad that Jesus came with a mission
and fulfilled it, aren't you?

We will discuss the turban further in a few pages, but for now I want to make the point that our minds must make what I refer to as a "violent turn" in our thinking. This is how we truly begin to renew our minds. As we head clearly down our path to healing, we must make a garment change, and the "turban" is part of that.

Precious believer, your garments of shame are about to be removed, and you are going to be reclothed as a holy priest of God.

A KEY PASSAGE FROM ZECHARIAH

We have learned that our Accuser is both sly and seductive. Remember that he is a whisperer and a familiar voice. In chapter 4, where we discussed the third lie of the Accuser ("Listen to My Whispers"), we saw how Satan accused God's holy priesthood in the third chapter of Zechariah. I want us to once again, but this time in greater detail, study the positioning of the Accuser and the garment change of the priesthood. This chapter has only ten verses, but each verse is pivotal to your personal increase and breakthrough. Take a few minutes now and read all ten verses, then we will walk through them together.

> Then he showed me Joshua the high priest standing before the angel of the LORD, and Satan standing at his right side to accuse him. The LORD said to Satan, "The LORD rebuke you, Satan! The LORD, who has chosen Jerusalem, rebuke you! Is not this man a burning stick snatched from the fire?"
> Now Joshua was dressed in filthy clothes as he stood before the angel. The angel said to those who were standing before him, "Take off his filthy clothes."
> Then he said to Joshua, "See, I have taken away your sin, and I will put rich garments on you."
> Then I said, "Put a clean turban on his head." So they put a clean turban on his head and clothed him, while the angel of the LORD stood by.

The angel of the LORD gave this charge to Joshua: "This is what the LORD Almighty says: 'If you will walk in my ways and keep my requirements, then you will govern my house and have charge of my courts, and I will give you a place among these standing here.

Listen, O high priest Joshua and your associates seated before you, who are men symbolic of things to come: I am going to bring my servant, the Branch. See, the stone I have set in front of Joshua! There are seven eyes on that one stone, and I will engrave an inscription on it,' says the LORD Almighty, 'and I will remove the sin of this land in a single day.

In that day each of you will invite his neighbor to sit under his vine and fig tree,' declares the LORD Almighty."

—ZECHARIAH 3:1–10

I have reprinted this entire passage here because it is so important for you to take the necessary time to properly position your spirit for God to empower you for change. Reading all of it will position you to break forth—body, soul and spirit. To simply read the revelation I personally receive is only a piece of the puzzle that leads to your completeness. The other puzzle pieces need to be given to you directly from the Holy Spirit. These passages will position you to break forth—body, soul and spirit.

Let's look back at the first two verses of this passage together as I highlight some key points:

1. **"Then he showed me Joshua the high priest standing before the angel of the LORD" (Zechariah 3:1). This passage clearly states that the high priest is standing before the angel of the Lord.**

Some theologians believe that the "angel of the Lord" in this passage is the Lord Himself. I agree with this opinion. Since we all are priests of the Lord, it bears more witness to me that when we are challenged in life the Lord stands with us. And at times we are brought before Him to examine our hearts and lives. I call these times opportunities for self-examination and repentance. Have you felt at times that you are standing before the Lord for examination?

When we are *before* the Lord, we are face-to-face. Now before you say we cannot see His face and live, let me just explain the Hebrew explanation for being *before* the Lord. The Hebrew word for *before* is *panah,* which means to "face, appear and to look."[2] It is the same word used in Genesis to describe how God moved upon the *face* of the deep and the *face* of the waters. In other words, He looked upon the potential of the darkness and the potential of the waters and the potential of the earth. Then He spoke, and things really changed.

When we meet God face-to-face, He looks upon the face of our potential. His Spirit broods over us—at all times—especially when we are ready for Him to speak into our future. When we stand *before* Him He looks at our *face value,* and then He prophesies into it. Regardless of what the devil says or how it looks in the natural, God speaks His divine will into our destiny.

2. **"And Satan [was] standing at his right side to accuse him" (Zechariah 3:1). Clearly, Satan, the Accuser, was standing immediately at the priest's right side in order to accuse him.**

What a picture this paints! Imagine yourself standing before God with the Accuser standing *right* beside you to falsely accuse you. Satan is incredibly good at falsely accusing us. The devil covets being right in the middle of our prayers to God and falsely accusing us each time we lift up a prayer. Perhaps at times you have been before the Lord and prayed, and suddenly you have heard a voice that said, "Who do you think you are? You cannot talk to God. You sinned today. In fact, you sinned as a child. You were molested when you were younger; you cannot talk to God."

3. **"The LORD said to Satan, 'The LORD rebuke you, Satan! The LORD, who has chosen Jerusalem, rebuke you!'" (Zechariah 3:2). Indeed, the Lord rebukes Satan, our Accuser. He has chosen us, and therefore He Himself, in His holiness, rebukes the Accuser.**

What an awesome thought! Because God has chosen us, He is therefore committed to rebuke the Accuser. Sure, we have sinned in the past. We may even have a particular recurring sin. But when the Lord looks at us, He sees the blood of Jesus. Jesus *died* for us to be chosen and forgiven. Because of the New Covenant, the Accuser has no say in the court of heaven. No matter what has caused your shame, God has chosen you.

4. **"'Is not this man a burning stick snatched from the fire?'" (Zechariah 3:2). The Lord realizes that we are burning sticks, or "firebrands," plucked from the fire.**

In Texas, cattle and livestock are selected from a herd and "marked" with a hot branding iron. It is the same with us as believers. God has chosen us and marked us as His own.

And, precious believer, God has plans for us. He wants to use *us* as branding irons. He desires to use us as a standard, to set the mark in the Spirit. He will use us to mark others for the Kingdom of Light as we testify to them of God's goodness.

Furthermore, we have been *snatched* from the fire. The Hebrew word for *snatched* is the word *natsal,* which means "delivered."[3] It is the same word that is used in the Bible to describe how God delivered Israel out of Egypt. Yes, dear ones, we have pressed through fiery trials and can still stand. Indeed, God saw us in the fire and then delivered us from it. The fire is necessary for *all* of us. The way to come out of the test with victory is to keep our hearts positioned before the Lord. This positions us to receive our new garments.

God sees our hearts. He has chosen us. We are His own.

THE GARMENT CHANGE

Now, let's shift into a supernatural dimension. God desires to make all things new, and He can empower us to leave the past behind.

One of the ways He does this is to renew our minds. Paul encourages us not to be "fashioned according to this world: but be ye transformed by the renewing of your mind, and ye may prove what is the good and acceptable and perfect will of God" (Romans 12:2, ASV).

As we saw in the last chapter, the way to become transformed is to renew our minds. The word *transformed* implies that we are changed into God's image. The change involves a renewing of our minds. I have always believed that the battle in spiritual warfare begins in the mind. Is it any wonder that the Accuser attacks our minds so often? Dear ones, if he can convince us to believe his lies, then he has won the battle. On the other hand, if we believe his lies, then we are never transformed into God's image.

God has had a plan all along to transform us. Let's not give the enemy too much credit. Although he is an ancient serpent who beguiled mankind from the beginning, he cannot stop us from achieving our destinies unless we determine not to receive our new garments of holiness.

How do we receive those new garments? Let's examine Zechariah 3 through 5 and scrutinize not only the garment change, but also the removal of the shame of the priesthood. Hang in there, dear ones; I want you to receive *all* God has for you.

1. **"Now Joshua was dressed in filthy clothes as he stood before the angel. The angel said to those who were standing before him, 'Take off his filthy clothes'" (Zechariah 3:3–4). Dear ones, the priesthood was dressed in filthy clothes, and God had them removed.**

Filthy clothes are garments of shame. When Zechariah wrote this message, the priesthood was tarnished with years of shame and defilement. And the sins of the priesthood had come face-to-face with the Lord. Instead of condemning them, the Lord said to "take off his filthy clothes" (his shame).

Precious believer, God does not reject us because of our past shame. In fact, He desires to restore us all the more and remove us from the pain of our past. He is forgiving our past and speaking into our future. As a sign, He is reclothing us. Hallelujah!

2. **"Then he said to Joshua, 'See, I have taken away your sin, and I will put rich garments on you.' Then I said, 'Put a clean turban on his head.' So they put a clean turban on his head and clothed him, while the angel of the LORD stood by" (Zechariah 3:4–5). We see here that God takes away our sin and replaces it with rich garments and a clean turban.**

Notice that God did not just command those before him to clothe him with garments; He had them clothe Joshua with *rich* garments. Garments are garments, but a *rich* one is worth some study. The King James Version of the Bible uses the words "change of raiment." The Hebrew word for this is *chalets,* which means "(again) to deliver, equip (for fight), present, and strengthen."[4] *Strong's* goes further to use the words "to arm (implying a soldier armed), make fat, loose, be ready and prepared."[5] These meanings imply that when God removes our shameful and "filthy" garments and replaces them with new "rich garments," He empowers us for warfare and arms us for battle. Who will we be empowered to battle? The Accuser. Why? Because he will attempt to lie to us again and say, "You are not worthy of a clean garment."

The meaning also speaks of deliverance. Dear ones, God has delivered us. He is binding up our brokenheartedness.

Now let's turn to the "clean turban." I feel I have written an entire chapter to get to this one point.

The Hebrew word for *turban* is the word *tsaniyph* (pronounced tsaw-neef), which means "a headdress" or "a hood."[6] It is linked to another Hebrew word, *tsanaph* (pronounced tsaw-naf), which means "to wrap, roll or dress."[7] If you remember, the word *turban* was one of the words used to define the words *bind up.* A turban, then, implies a binding of something to the head.

Our brains—our minds—have been defiled by the Accuser's lies. Yet our God wants to deliver us from the lies the enemy has spoken. God wants to remove the filthy garments of shame that have covered our minds.

And dear ones, the mind and the heart are connected. As a man thinks in his heart, so is he. If our hearts need healing, then, so do our minds. Jesus came to "bind up" the brokenhearted, did He not?

But, there is just one more thing—and you must understand this, or I feel that all I have written will have been in vain. Another definition of *turban* is "to violently turn."[8] Did you get that? We have to make a violent turn in our minds in order to defeat the Accuser.

Think of how a turban is bound up. A turban is wrapped securely to the head. Radical folds and turns are made as the turban is wrapped. Could it be that to receive a clean mind concerning our future and destiny we must make a violent turn toward God and His Word?

Believers, unless we come into complete agreement with His Word, then we cannot move forward and completely defeat our Accuser. The Lord has much for us to do as we build His Kingdom.

INVENTORY TIME

Let's take a short break here. It is inventory time once more. I ask you to take a little time to write down a few thoughts that will empower you to shift into your garment change.

Come before the Lord, and ask Him if you have settled for less than His best for you. Do you have mindsets concerning your potential? Do you believe that shame has held you back from seeking God's best?

1. Name any areas of your life that need healing and restoration.

2. Name any areas in which you continually experience pain, weakness and shame.

3. Fill in the blank: The Accuser has deceived you with the following lie: "You can't have a relationship with God because you _____."

4. Describe any ways in which the Accuser is lying to you right now, even as you are praying to the Father.

Now let's lift all of these things up to the Lord. Ask Him right now to take away your garments of shame and replace them with His rich garments and clean turban. He will do it, dear one. He is faithful.

Now allow me to pray for you:

Lord, I pray for these precious children of Yours to under-stand fully the ways of the Accuser. But more than that, I ask that You reveal Yourself to them and empower them with Your stead-fast love. As they continue to study and forge ahead, I thank You that You are removing old garments of shame. I declare that they will not become overwhelmed but that a supernatural rest will cover them. Isaiah 58:8 says that "Your light shall break forth like the morning, Your healing shall spring forth speedily" (NKJV). I declare that You are healing these readers of any memories, pain or trauma of their past that attempts to block them from their victories in life. I also declare that the Accuser has no more influ-ence in their lives based on their history. Isaiah 58:8 continues to declare that You are their "rear guard" and You shall protect them as they continue to move forward into their futures. I pray that You are renewing their minds and that they are moving from strength to strength, glory to glory and faith to faith. In the name of Jesus, Amen.

THE CHARGE

Let's take just one more step to be empowered, shall we? After the garment change, the Lord charged Joshua by saying:

> Thus saith the LORD of hosts; If thou wilt walk in my ways, and if thou wilt keep my charge, then thou shalt also judge my house, and shalt also keep my courts, and I will give thee places to walk among these that stand by.
>
> —ZECHARIAH 3:3–7, KJV

God has a charge for you, too, dear one. He has a place for you, and He wants you to fulfill your divine potential.

Precious believer, see yourself clothed in your rich garment, completely delivered from the shame of your past. No longer can fear, trauma, pain, rejection or *anything* hold you back. You have both feet on the freedom road now; do not stop moving forward. God is with you.

I am so proud of you. It would have been easy for you to stop a few chapters back. The Accuser does not give up easily; I am sure you have noticed. But God believes in you, and so do I. Let's continue to walk through the remaining chapters together. Remember, I have prayed for you in advance. And even better: The Lord is with you every step of the way.

7

Lie #6:
SEAT ME IN YOUR HIGH PLACE

Then I heard a loud voice shouting across the heavens, "It has happened at last—the salvation and power and kingdom of our God, and the authority of His Christ. For the Accuser of our brothers and sisters has been thrown down to earth—the one who accuses them before our God day and night. And they have defeated him because of the blood of the Lamb and because of their testimony. And they did not love their lives so much that they were afraid to die."

REVELATION 12:10–11, NLT

Wouldn't you just love to witness with your own eyes the enemy being thrown down and defeated? Well, dear one, you will. God has already promised that "the Accuser . . . has been thrown down to earth" and that "they [we] have defeated him." Hallelujah!

But you do not have to wait until the last days to see the defeat of your enemy; the Accuser can be thrown from your life now. In chapter 5, we discussed that the kingdom of darkness has principalities, powers and rulers that have established themselves in "high places." In spiritual warfare, our goal is to expose Satan's plans to remain in an exalted position in our lives and then to tear him down.

> For we wrestle not against flesh and blood, but against principalities, against powers, against the rulers of the darkness of this world, against spiritual wickedness in high places.
>
> —EPHESIANS 6:12, KJV

Every high thing in our lives that is not of the Lord needs to be thrown (or torn) down. I am certain that as you continue to break free from the Accuser, you will witness the enemy of your life being thrown down. When the enemy is cast down from his seated position, we can say, as John the Revelator once witnessed in a vision, "It has happened at last." Can you envision it also?

Listen, dear ones: The freer we become, the more the enemy is dethroned. I want to see him fall from his idolatrous position in my life; don't you feel the same? If you read this chapter with a determination to see the Accuser cast out of your life, then you will witness such freedom.

I am sure that you are on the same journey as I am—attempting to move from "here" to arrive at "there."

Precious believers, the only difference between "here" and "there" is the letter "T." You have come to a "T" in your road. You can become frustrated, decide to stop now and put down this book, or you can press on a little further and find freedom. The devil—your Accuser—is active even now. He has tried to stop you from reading thus far—I am certain of it. And he will try even harder now, for he does not want you to cast him out. He feels he has a safe place living in your life, and he will do all he can to maintain that high position. Don't let him. Press on with me as we lay a firm foundation from which you will be empowered to launch into freedom. Remember that Satan's goal is to get even with God by targeting those whom God loves—you and me. Let's make a radical turn toward God and claim our new garment and new turban. Satan will be defeated, and we will be the winners in this battle. Let's tear him down out of our high places.

REVELATION'S CLUES FOR OVERCOMING

Let's examine Revelation 12:10–11 more closely to see how Scripture describes the Accuser who is cast down and defeated by Christ's authority. The Savior desires to reveal so much to us in this passage, especially in regard to how we, as believers, can also defeat this false Accuser. I hope to pour life into the words I use to describe what I see in this passage.

Verse 10 says that the Accuser accuses us before God day and night. This is one of his tactics; he is relentless. I cannot help but wonder how the devil has so much energy, especially when he knows what the final result will be. How can he not just give up, knowing that Christ has already won the victory over him? The answer is that Satan hates God so much that even though he knows he is defeated, he will continue to accuse God's people until the very last moment.

How do we overcome him? By three things:

1. The blood of the Lamb.

"And they have defeated him by the blood of the Lamb" (Revelation 12:11, TLB).

If we are born again, then we are removed from our sin. The blood of Jesus has saved us and delivered us from the Accuser. In this passage in Revelation, the blood of Christ is listed first as a method of defeat. It is, therefore, the most powerful way to defeat the Accuser. We will discuss more about the blood of Christ in chapter 9. For now, let's recognize the fact that because we are saved we are covered with the blood of Jesus, which conquers our adversary. By Christ's dying, the Accuser is destroyed. Yes, Christ has destroyed the one who had the power of death. The Accuser is already defeated.

2. The word of our testimony.

"And by the word of their testimony" (Revelation 12:11).

We can use our testimonies against the Accuser. When we speak the Word of God concerning a situation, the enemy is cast out. When we speak our testimonies, we are using God's Word—the testimony of His faithfulness and our promised victory. We must preach, teach, declare and pull down strongholds with our testimonies. And when evidence of victory comes, we should stand up and give God glory. This entire book is devoted to developing a testimony of overcoming the Accuser.

3. Loving not our own lives unto death.

"And they did not love their lives so much that they were afraid to die" (Revelation 12:11).

In any war, there is the opportunity for death. We must constantly die to ourselves. We must continually lay down our lives and follow Christ. On the surface it might appear that we are giving up everything—and we are—but the amazing thing is that when we lay down everything, we come out on top. We are victorious. We overcome our Accuser.

We never fail God's tests; we just take them again until we pass them. In the midst of suffering we must be patient and allow God to work His perfection in us during our trials. In the process, we must have courage and faith in God and die daily. This death to self and our selfish ambition defeats the Accuser.

Precious believer, what has to die in you so that you are able to embrace end-time strategies to defeat the Accuser? Pride? Ego? Control? My answers would be yes, yes and yes. God is still perfecting the Sandie that is destined to be "Freed."

GOD ALLOWS THE ACCUSER MORE TIME

Unfortunately, God has allowed the Accuser a little more time. Why does the Lord do this?

God is using Satan. Yes, the Accuser is being used. God uses the enemy to prove us.

You see, God gives Satan time to test us so that *we* know what is really deep down inside of us. As I said when we studied Job, God knew all along that Job would pass the test. Job, however, did not know how strong he was until he had some competition. Competition in sports makes our bodies strong. It is the same in the spiritual realm. Opposition from our enemy makes us spiritually strong. Deep down inside each of us is a warrior, a victor, who knows who he is and Whose he is.

Let's look at the verse that follows the passage in Revelation we have been discussing. In Revelation 12:12, John says:

> Rejoice, O heavens! And you who live in the heavens, rejoice! But terror will come on the earth and the sea. For the Devil has come down to you in great anger, and he knows that he has little time. (NLT)

I hate that part, don't you? The enemy is angry at us and at God, and he comes down with all of that awful anger because he knows he has little time. As evil as he is, he is not stupid. He is a strong adversary in every way. But a good opponent brings out the muscle in all of us. The fire is getting hotter; the temperature is rising; yet we are being empowered with an end-time overcomer's anointing to cast out the devil.

Sometimes when I am battling the Accuser, I know I must look rather comical to God. At such times I inevitably attempt to go to battle without spending time in prayer and gaining godly strategy. I can just picture Him sitting on His throne, observing me and chuckling as I attempt to "sucker punch" the enemy in my own strength. I usually end up taking a swing and falling flat. With His grace, I am able to get up again. Finally I ask Him for a present-day strategy.

Only God can empower me with this type of ammunition. Only a heavenly plan will empower us for these end times. For more information about gaining present-day strategies from the Lord to defeat the Accuser, I encourage you to read my book *Strategies from Heaven's Throne*.

THE EXAMPLE JESUS SET FOR CASTING OUT THE ACCUSER

The entire ministry of Jesus focused on *casting out* demons. One in particular with which I am amazed is found in Matthew 8:15–16. Jesus had just healed Peter's mother-in-law from an acute illness with fever. He merely reached out and touched her hand and she arose instantly, completely healed. And then, "When evening was come, they brought unto Him many possessed with demons: and He *cast out the spirits with a word*, and healed all that were sick" (Matthew 8:16, asv, emphasis mine).

Notice my emphasis: Jesus *cast out the spirits* (the demons) *with a word*. The Greek word used here for *word* is *logos*, which translates as "the Word of God." I do not know what part of God's Word (*logos*) He said. I am sure He said exactly what the Father instructed Him to say. But whatever it was, Jesus cast out the demons with a *logos* revelation—a revelation that resulted in a Word from God that set others free.

Dear ones, we have this same power. We can speak the Word of God with our authority in Christ, and demons have to flee. Yes, the enemy can be *cast out* of our lives. We can defeat the Accuser.

Understanding the tactics of our enemy and how to defeat him is a form of revelation from heaven. This is one reason why I continue to write. I want each believer empowered, equipped and ready for battle. I hate the devil, and I want to see him thrown down and defeated. I pray that I am a vessel God uses to disclose to you the mysteries of His Kingdom and to defeat the kingdom of darkness in your life.

DOUBT AND UNBELIEF

It is sad for me to admit that after almost five decades of knowing Jesus, I am just now understanding the magnitude of one particular sin: unbelief. I fear I am not alone in this walk of fully trusting God.

In Mark 9:16–19, a man brought his demon-possessed son to Jesus. He had first brought him to the disciples to cast out the demons, but they were not successful, so the man came to Jesus Himself. Jesus was grieved that His disciples could not cast out the demons, and He referred to them as an *unbelieving generation:* "'O *unbelieving generation,*' Jesus replied, 'how long shall I stay with you? How long shall I put up with you? Bring the boy to me'" (Mark 9:19, emphasis mine). Jesus then healed the boy.

The Greek word for *unbelieving* in this passage implies that when we have little faith, then we have no "confidence" in Christ. In other words, we conclude that Jesus is untrustworthy. Ouch. That is almost too difficult to write. Yet, I am guilty of this sin at times. Scripture says that, "He that covereth his sin shall not prosper."

Beloved, now is the time to " 'fess up" if we desire to prosper. I encourage you to consider areas of your life in which you have not had enough confidence in Christ. Repent of any areas where you have doubted God or not believed fully in Him.

When the Accuser hits hard, you can bet it will be with a blow that will test your faith in God's steadfast Word. Philippians 3:3 warns us about putting our *confidence* in the flesh. Our fleshly responses during difficult times will dictate our future in a negative way. We are encouraged by God to have confidence in Him.

The word *confidence* is a Hebrew word, *kacal*, which is connected to the Hebrew word "anointing."[1] We can actually say that we should trust in the Lord and His anointing to provide, heal, restore and deliver us—from *any and every* demon and the Accuser's lies concerning us, our families, our businesses and our futures. On the other hand, we can conclude that if we do not trust in His anointing, then the enemy will gain a stronghold over us.

OVERCOMING SOME SPECIFIC LIES OF THE ACCUSER

Remember that part of overcoming the Accuser is to speak God's Word over the accusation. Allow me to empower you today with some biblical promises from your Father God that negate several specific lies of your Accuser.

1.	**Lie**	The Accuser says: "You are going to get sick and die."
	Truth	God's Word says: "Have no fear of sudden disaster or of the ruin that overtakes the wicked, for the LORD will be your confidence and will keep your foot from being snared" (Proverbs 3:25–26).

2.	Lie	The Accuser says: "Your life is unstable. Finances are unpredictable. What about your future?"
	Truth	God's Word says: "But blessed is the man who trusts in the LORD, whose confidence is in him. He will be like a tree planted by the water that sends out its roots by the stream. It does not fear when heat comes; its leaves are always green. It has no worries in a year of drought and never fails to bear fruit" (Jeremiah 17:7–8).
3.	Lie	The Accuser says: "God is unapproachable. He is not concerned with your problems and your present suffering."
	Truth	The apostle Paul wrote: "In him and through faith in him we may approach God with freedom and confidence. I ask you, therefore, not to be discouraged because of my sufferings for you, which are your glory" (Ephesians 3:12–13).
4.	Lie	The Accuser says: "God will not help us in our time of need."
	Truth	God promises: "Let us then approach the throne of grace with confidence, so that we may receive mercy and find grace to help us in our time of need" (Hebrews 4:16).
5.	Lie	The Accuser says: "You will never change. You are a sinner. God has not provided salvation and redemption for you."
	Truth	God says: "Therefore, brothers, since we have confidence to enter the Most Holy Place by the blood of Jesus, by a new and living way opened for us through the curtain, that is, his body, and since we have a great priest over the house of God, let us draw near to God with a sincere heart in full assurance of faith, having our hearts sprinkled to cleanse us from a guilty conscience and having our bodies washed with pure water" (Hebrews 10:19–22).
6.	Lie	The Accuser says: "You cannot make it. Throw in the towel. Quit. God will not prove to be faithful."
	Truth	God encourages us: "So do not throw away your confidence; it will be richly rewarded. You need to persevere so that when you have done the will of God, you will receive what he has promised" (Hebrews 10:35–36).

| 7. | Lie | The Accuser says: "You are alone. You are abandoned. There is no one to help you." |
| | Truth | God tells us: "So we say with confidence, 'The Lord is my helper; I will not be afraid. What can man do to me?' " (Hebrews 13:6). |

You might be interested to learn that the word *helper* (Hebrew: *halal*) in this last passage means "to cry out for help" and is connected to the word "hallelujah."[2] It also means "to praise" and "to give a clear sharp sound in rejoicing." I believe Jesus rejoices each time He can confidently rescue us. Each time we cry out for Him, He gets excited and celebrates the opportunity to rescue us from our Accuser. Dear believer, all we have to do is ask for help, and He moves heaven and earth to empower us for victory.

Hallelujah!

| 8. | Lie | The Accuser says: "God does not love you." The Accuser also will tempt you to fear. |
| | Truth | God's Word says: "God is love. Whoever lives in love lives in God, and God in him. In this way, love is made complete among us so that we will have confidence on the day of judgment, because in this world we are like him. There is no fear in love. But perfect love drives out fear, because fear has to do with punishment. The one who fears is not made perfect in love" (1 John 4:16–18). |

In this chapter I have given you eight specific, common lies of the Accuser (not to be confused with the seven broader lies that are the heart of this book and are encompassed in the titles of chapters 2 through 8). I have paired these eight specific lies with eight Scriptures to build your faith. Are there other lies the Accuser is trying to lead you to believe as he seeks that exalted position in your life? Is your enemy causing you to doubt God's faithfulness and ability to heal and deliver you? The Accuser will always attempt to rob your trust in God's faithfulness and His desire to restore you.

I encourage you now to write down other lies the Accuser is whispering to you and to search God's Word for Scriptures with which to overcome those lies. I promise you God's Word contains the truths that will defeat our enemy. And when we speak that Word over a situation in our lives, we dethrone Satan from his (assumed) exalted position.

TAKE THE NEXT STEP

It is time to take the next step. In order to tear down Satan's high place in your life, you must forgive yourself for your past. Remember that the Accuser would like to step in here as you are almost finished with this book. He would like to prevent you from putting the old season behind you. He would like to gain another foothold in your life. Yet the Holy Spirit is so much smarter than he.

As you seek to forgive yourself, I want you to know that there is *nothing* you could ever do that would cause Christ Jesus to stop loving you. Imagine Christ's crucifixion. Though it is always difficult to go there in your mind's eye, I want you to picture what the Savior endured so that you do not have to surrender to the lies of the Accuser.

Jesus died with forgiveness. He forgave others for their false accusations, even with His dying breaths. Dear one, He was forgiving you. It is impossible to imagine how He could do this—how full of love His heart must have been for you that He could be thinking of sinful you even in the midst of such unimaginable pain.

If the Savior of the world can forgive you in such a powerful way, then can you not forgive yourself? Can you forgive yourself for doubting God? Can you forgive yourself for your past? Can you forgive yourself for what you have done to others?

Often in my life I have felt that God's forgiveness was not free. I wish I had understood earlier in my life that His forgiveness *is* free to those who believe and ask for it. We cannot pay for it; Jesus would not allow that. Instead, He chose to give His life for our freedom.

Beloved, it is time to run to the cross. Go to His mercy seat and ask for His mercy, yet also believe that He is giving you grace for your future. Ask Him to cause your heart to burn for Him again. Receive His forgiveness and freedom today.

I encourage you just to spend a little time with Him right now and let the perfect, complete, loving forgiveness of Jesus soak into your heart. . . .

Now, dear one, begin to boldly declare to the devil that you have the mind of Christ and that no weapon that he forms against you will prosper. Commit today to continue to renew your mind, embracing God's truth and rejecting Satan's lies. Just lift your hands and receive it from the Lord right now: "Lord, empower me with an end-time overcoming anointing. I receive it."

SALVATION, POWER AND THE KINGDOM OF OUR GOD

It is our responsibility to use our blood-bought authority to cast the devil out of our lives. We can no longer allow Satan to have a seated position—a seat of authority—over us. We can no longer let the devil falsely accuse us. We cannot be like the church of Pergamos, which allowed Satan to have a seated position over them (see Revelation 2:12–13), for the Lord rebuked them for allowing a demonic structure to be erected there.

In one of my recent books, *Conquering the Antichrist Spirit: Discerning and Defeating the Seducer That Binds Believers Today*,[3] I give an example from the book of Daniel that is relevant to mention here because it concerns dethroning the enemy. In Daniel 7, God gives the prophet a dream in which he clearly sees God's courtroom in heaven:

> As I looked, thrones were set in place, and the Ancient of Days took his seat. His clothing was as white as snow; the hair of his head was white like wool. His throne was flaming with fire, and its wheels were all ablaze. A river of fire was flowing, coming out from before him. Thousands upon thousands attended him; ten thousand times ten thousand stood before him. The court was seated, and the books were opened. . . . *I kept looking until the beast was slain and its body destroyed and thrown into the blazing fire.* . . . In my vision at night I looked, and there before me was one like a son of man, coming with the clouds of heaven. He approached the Ancient of Days and was led into his presence. He was given authority, glory and sovereign power; all peoples, nations and men of every language worshiped him. His dominion is an everlasting dominion that will not pass away, and his kingdom is one that will never be destroyed.
>
> —DANIEL 7:9–14 (EMPHASIS MINE)

The King James Version says that as Daniel watched in his dream, "thrones were cast down." In a spiritual sense, I believe this passage means that all demonic thrones—the false voices, false and demonically inspired leaders and demonic positions of authority (high places)—were cast down, and godly authority was put into proper positioning. Why? Because the Ancient of Days walked into the courtroom.

Believers, when God shows up to righteously judge your situation, He sees the Accuser who falsely accuses you and is committed to casting him out of your life because of the blood of Jesus. Satan has attempted to exalt his words above God. *But when heaven comes to earth, so does God's government.* He is the King above all kings. God loves to "punch out the devil's lights," and He enjoys using us to do this for Him. And dear ones, we cannot cast down the devil without God's leading and strategy.

Because of the blood of Jesus, we have salvation—and this includes salvation from our Accuser. Jesus' work for us on the cross and the gift of His Holy Spirit also gives us the power to overcome our Accuser and throw him out of our high places. Finally, when we do so, the Kingdom of the Most High God reigns in our lives.

LET'S CELEBRATE

In Revelation 12:10, the apostle John uses a celebratory tone. In the form of a triumphant song, John gives a magnificent testimony of an adored conqueror, Christ Jesus, who has won the battle against the Accuser and established salvation, strength and the Kingdom of our God. Christ's power and authority has *cast down* the Accuser. It is as if John is joyfully singing, "Hallelujah! Praise the Lord! Finally, the Accuser is thrown down to earth, and the salvation, along with the power of God and His Kingdom, are being established. God has shown Himself to be a mighty God, and Christ has shown Himself to be a strong and mighty Savior. By His own arm He has brought salvation, and now His eternal Kingdom will become greatly increased and established." John's praise makes us want to rise up and sing right along with him.

Indeed, when Satan is cast into the fiery pit because none of his accusations can stand, we will rise up and sing. We, along with God's people from the beginning of time, will rejoice with Christ that we stand blameless, washed in His blood. But, believers, we can feel that same joy now. We can overcome the Accuser and tear down his seated positions in our own lives right now—today—and allow the Lord back into our high places.

8

Lie #7:
GOD DOES NOT REMEMBER YOU

Then God remembered Rachel, and answered her pleading, and made it possible for her to have children.

GENESIS 30:22, AMP

Rachel sat in the shade, watching the sun begin to melt into the darkness of evening. She fidgeted with her garment, retied her roped belt around her narrow waist and gently swept her hair back from her exquisite face.

Rachel had always been beautiful. Her whole life, she had always drawn more attention than her older sister, Leah. Leah's eyes were weak-looking, and this was considered by many to be a blemish. Leah did not measure up to their cultural standards of beauty. Rachel did, and this fact had caused problems for the two sisters when they were younger. It still did.

Today Rachel thought of the unique beauty she had had since

her youth. She remembered as a child catching slight glimpses of herself as the sun reflected her image in the well while she drew water for her father's sheep. Years ago Jacob had given her a tiny but costly hand mirror made of highly polished mixed metals, chiefly copper. Rachel was extremely proud and possessive of this treasure, and sometimes she even wore it on a chain around her neck, for it was quite ornamental. As the sun disappeared behind the horizon and the moon partially lit the sky, Rachel turned the mirror upward toward her face, attempting to catch enough moonlight to reflect upon it. When the mirror caught the moon's rays, Rachel gazed at her seemingly timeless beauty.

Do I still appeal to my husband? Has my beauty faded, just as the sun hides itself at the end of day? How can I draw him closer again? Tossing her head from side to side, Rachel became lost in her thoughts. She wondered if Jacob had regretted the years of labor he committed to Laban in order to marry her. If so, did he still love her? *Yet how could he love me, a woman cursed with barrenness?* Rachel worked to refocus her thoughts, but tonight it was impossible. The Accuser was working overtime. Her mind was flooded with words such as "shameful, failure, hopeless, barren, unattractive, abandoned and unwanted."

Will he visit me tonight? She sighed, not knowing. Rachel longed for Jacob's touch, his tender words and his gentle caress. But she needed more from him. Rachel needed a son.

Her womb closed, Rachel was marked with shame. The curse of barrenness that was etched upon her heart deepened daily as she watched her sister, Leah, parade her many children past Rachel's tent day after day, night after night. These two sisters were embroiled in stiff competition. Each did all she could to manipulate the husband they shared into obtaining what she wanted from him—and what each wanted from Jacob was children. Just how low each would stoop to become fruitful was yet to be determined.

The Accuser was fully active as he falsely accused each of these sisters. Leah was constantly reminded that Jacob preferred Rachel's beauty. Rachel, though more loved by Jacob from the time they met, was tortured by her barrenness, and the Accuser was relentless in lying to her concerning her self-worth. The devil also pitted the sisters against each other with his manipulation and lies. Leah became prideful about her seemingly endless ability to produce heirs for Jacob. Rachel's jealousy and feelings of inadequacy filled her to overflowing. Being sisters no longer demanded any level of loyalty; each sister was out for herself. Yes, both sisters daily fought the Accuser, the unseen enemy who continually spoke into their minds with his false accusations. Both women struggled with depression, despair, jealousy, competition and fear of rejection, and the Accuser always knew which buttons to push for each of them.

It had been a particularly difficult day for Rachel. She had tangled with Leah this morning. It seemed as if Leah was always reminding Rachel of her barrenness. That morning Leah had even deliberately accused Rachel of being "unwanted, undesirable, unworthy, unfit" and certainly "cursed." These words had cut Rachel to her already wounded and bleeding heart. Could these words really have come from her own flesh and blood?

Rachel walked toward the pasture where Jacob's sheep were feeding. She watched Jacob begin to gather the sheep into the protective fold for the night. Oh, how she loved her husband. She remembered fondly the first time she saw him at the well near her father's home. She had been tending her father's sheep that day. It seemed just an ordinary day, but it proved to be a day of providence.

As Rachel continued to wait for Jacob, her mind filled with more memories. She recalled Jacob's story of his experience at Bethel, the place where he had encountered the Lord face-to-face. Rachel knew that on that divine night God had promised Jacob many descendants. Jacob had told her that God "stood over and beside him and said, I am the Lord, the God of Abraham your father [forefather] and the God of Isaac; I will give to you and to your descendants the land on which you are lying" (Genesis 28:13, AMP). God also had promised Jacob that his offspring "shall be as [countless as] the dust or sand of the ground . . . and by you and your Offspring shall all the families of the earth be blessed and bless themselves" (verse 14).

Rachel felt tears forming again. "Why aren't I blessed with one of his offspring?" she said out loud. "God promised my husband an abundance of children. Leah is getting older. Surely she cannot fill the earth with all those children by herself." Rachel angrily stomped her feet and kicked at the dirt, caking her sandals and dainty feet with the sandy soil.

Rachel's frustrated words caught Jacob's attention. From his position near the sheep fold, he could hear her voice but not the words she spoke, and her anger alarmed him. "Rachel, are you okay? Did you say something to me?" Closing the gate behind the last sheep, Jacob began to make his way toward her. Though her long robe covered her feet, she reached down to tidy her sandals and feet as he came closer. She grew nervous with each of his steps.

The Accuser was on the alert. His goal was to rob Rachel of her hope, and he had become entrenched in Rachel's thoughts as he continually spoke words of shame. Knowing that despair blocks destiny and would render her helpless, the Accuser whispered into Rachel's ear: "Jacob does not want to lie with you tonight. Leah is the only one who can give him children. Just give up; quit trying to make something of this relationship that is not there."

Rachel's heart was gripped with fear. *I hope he does not reject me. I do not think I can handle it—not tonight of all nights.*

Jacob stood beside Rachel and caressed her tenderly. "Tears, my love? May I question why?" Jacob wiped her tear-stained face with the edge of his garment.

"Dearest husband, I must have children or I will die!" Rachel began to weep out loud, her tears flowing uncontrollably. "Will you lie with me tonight?" Her sad red eyes met his.

Jacob sighed and looked down at the ground. He let out another sigh as he struggled to answer. "No, Rachel. I am sorry. I promised Leah three more days. I believe it may be her timing to conceive. I will lie with you after my time with her."

Rachel could not respond. She looked down at the dirt and bit her lip. Her heart felt as if it would break. She wanted to flee. Indeed, she wanted to die.

Jacob saw her pain. He gently took her face in his hands and lifted her head until her eyes met his. He adored Rachel's strong eyes; they were what caught his attention from the time they met at her father's well. Leah's eyes were weak and did not speak to him as Rachel's did. As he looked upon them, he fell in love with her all over again.

"Now, you know you are the one I truly love. I have loved you from the moment I laid eyes on you."

Rachel struggled to get the words out. Her anger was fueled with accusing words. "Well, that's what you say. But you ended up with Leah first." Rachel pulled away, turning her back to Jacob and burying her face in her hands.

"Now, Rachel, you know the deception behind that." Jacob defended himself, yet his heart was full of compassion for his wife. His voice remained soft yet matter-of-fact. "Your father deliberately switched you with Leah on the wedding night—and after I had worked seven years for him thinking I was to marry you. You know that. After I consummated the marriage with Leah, I had to remain her husband. And then I worked seven more years so that your father would let me have you as my wife, too. You were the bride I always wanted, my Rachel. Now turn around and look at me so that we can talk about this and work through it."

Rachel maintained her position. "It's just not fair. I do not understand why your God would allow me to be in so much pain." Rachel began to regain her composure, but still needed to be heard. "You must give me children, Jacob, or else I will die."

Jacob reached out to turn her toward him, but Rachel blocked him with her hand. He then stepped in front of her and wrapped his arms tenderly around her, gently pressing her head against his strong shoulder. Rachel finally began to melt in his embrace.

"Now we must not falsely accuse God for causing our heartache," Jacob said. "He has made His covenant to bless me and my generations. And besides, we are married now. You know that I worked hard for your father for seven more years after his devious trick, so that he would bless me with you as my wife. Rachel, God promises to work all things for our good. We must stand on the promises that God has made with me and trust that He will remember His covenant."

Rachel lifted her eyes to meet his again. "I know. But my womb has begun to shrivel and dry up. I am so ashamed. I cannot control my thoughts. I feel as if I am cursed. I walk in shame every day, and I feel depressed. Each day I see Leah my mind is filled with tormenting thoughts. I believe that deep down inside I am being accused and condemned for something I cannot control." Rachel's tears flooded again as she poured out her heart to her husband.

"I understand, my love. I do. But do not allow your mind to control your actions. Your thoughts can falsely accuse you."

"Well, look at the facts. The accusations are true. I am barren, and Leah is not. Leah has had child after child during these many years. I have nothing." Rachel's pain was overriding her faith in God's timing and Jacob's patience to comfort her. Jacob tried once more to take her face in his strong hands, but Rachel pulled away. Rachel walked back to her tent—alone—and Jacob turned toward the tent of her sister once more.

Within a few minutes, Rachel was sobbing again. Inside her tent, her eyes fell upon the empty bowl that had held the mandrakes. *Mandrakes. I bet Leah sent Reuben out for those love apples again. Maybe if I can find some more mandrakes?*

Mandrakes were a weed found in the fields, and it was believed that they had special powers of fertility. Her nephew, Reuben, had found some mandrakes several weeks ago and had brought them to his mother, Leah. When Rachel discovered that Leah had mandrakes, she panicked. She went to Leah and convinced her sister to give the mandrakes to her in exchange for a night with Jacob. Rachel was so desperate to conceive that she willingly gave up a night of intimacy with Jacob in order to possess the mandrakes. Of course, Rachel was cursed yet again, as Leah was blessed that night to conceive another child (see Genesis 30:14–19).

She already has so many children. Rachel pounded her fist in her hand and wondered where she could find more mandrakes.

Rachel's mind was desperate, and she wondered what else she could do. She thought of Jacob's God, Jehovah. She had embraced Jacob's God but did not yet fully know His faithfulness. *Where is His faithfulness to me?* she wondered. *Why is it that only my sister is blessed with children?* The more Rachel focused on her shame, the more her thoughts fueled the Accuser until her mind was totally captivated by the words of her enemy: "Why don't you just go back to your father's idols? You were happier when you bowed down to them. You know where to find his idols. Go look in his tent; Laban still worships them."

Maybe it was better then, Rachel thought. *When I called upon my father's gods, I think they heard me.*

The Accuser's voice grew louder: "Go now, and bow down to them. You were happier then. You did not know shame until Jacob's God cursed you with barrenness. Your life has been miserable since you began to worship Jehovah."

Rachel started to change direction and head toward her father's tent, but then stopped. "No. I must not." Rachel put her hands to her mouth to control her words and actions, then ran as fast as her legs would support her to her tent. *Help me, Lord,* she prayed, *not to bow down to any false voice or false image.*

Rachel made the right choice. Although she was tormented by the Accuser, she did not bow down to him. She chose to believe God and not go back to what appeared more comfortable, more certain or more promising to her flesh and her own understanding.

And because of her choice, God remembered Rachel:

> Then God remembered Rachel, and answered her plead-
> ing, and made it possible for her to have children. And [now
> for the first time] she became pregnant and bore a son; and
> she said, God has taken away my reproach, disgrace and
> humiliation. And she called his name Joseph [may he add]
> and said, May the Lord add to me another son.
>
> —GENESIS 30:22–24, AMP

GOD REMEMBERED RACHEL

I have chosen to focus mostly on Rachel here for several reasons. First, I relate to Rachel and her broken heart. Second, I love this story because it is such a powerful reminder that God never forgets His promises. And third, Rachel's story teaches us that in His own time and in His season, God does remember us. While we will focus primarily on Rachel in this chapter, we will eventually circle back and revisit Leah in the next chapter.

As we begin our discussion of Rachel's story, we will focus on the importance of remembering. The word *remember* in this passage in Genesis is the Hebrew word *zakar*. It is a primitive root word, and according to *Strong's* it means "to (do something) properly; to mark; to remember, by implication; and to mention."[1] The original meaning of this word indicates that God *marked* Rachel with pregnancy. His mark of favor produced a transformation in her physical body, as well as a shift within her circumstances.

Rachel had felt abandoned and stuck in a prison with no hope of escape. Can you even imagine the torment she faced on a daily basis from the Accuser? If you have suffered with infertility, I know this is near to your heart and that you have ached with that same pain. But for those who have not experienced the agony of barrenness, it is difficult to imagine the incredible suffering Rachel lived through on a daily basis.

Yet we can imagine how the Accuser tortured her. Though the Accuser is not mentioned in the biblical account of Rachel, we know that he has been active since Satan was the worship leader in heaven, even before the creation of the world. It is obvious that he was alert and active in Rachel's life.

Deep within Rachel's heart was such a desire to bear children that she would have done *anything* to have them—manipulate, control, even lie if necessary. These were prime opportunities for her Accuser.

Yet Rachel remained faithful to the Lord. She *remembered* God's faithfulness and chose not to bow down to the false image of her Accuser. And, indeed, God was faithful to Rachel:

> Then God *remembered* Rachel, and answered her pleading, and made it possible for her to have children. And [now for the first time] she became pregnant and bore a son; and she said, God has taken away my reproach, disgrace and humiliation. And she called his name Joseph [may he add] and said, "May the Lord add to me another son."
>
> —GENESIS 30:22–24, AMP (EMPHASIS MINE)

God *remembered* Rachel and empowered her to move forward and fulfill her divine destiny. God promises always to *remember* us. He promises to seal our faith and connect us securely to our covenant with Him.

When God *remembered* Rachel, action was taken. God's *remembrance* of Rachel led to her conception and proved His faithfulness to deliver His child from barrenness. As God marked Rachel with fruitfulness and success, so He also desires to remember us. Yes, dear ones, He desires for us to be fruitful and to increase, too.

BACKTRACKING TOWARD THE ACCUSER

While Rachel maintained her faith in Jehovah as best she could before her conception, not long after her miracle she listened to the Accuser and backtracked. Genesis 31 describes how the Lord later told Jacob to return to the land of his fathers (the Promised Land). While he and his family were packing and Rachel and Leah's father, Laban, was in the fields with the sheep, Rachel stole into her father's tent, took her father's idols and hid them in her camel's saddle. Then she sat on them. Later, she even lied to her father, telling him that she could not rise to greet him. Laban looked everywhere for his idols—in Jacob's tent, Leah's tent, in Rachel's tent and in the tent of the maids.

The Bible does not tell us exactly why Rachel stole the idols. Perhaps she stole them from her father out of fear that he might consult them as to where Jacob fled after he left Laban. Perhaps she was just struggling with leaving her past behind. These idols had probably been her "gods" all her life until meeting Jacob. Rachel *remembered* them, and she did not want to leave them behind. I would guess that many times Rachel battled a temptation to go back in her faith to what she believed to be better.

Jacob, not knowing it was Rachel who had taken the idols, pronounced a curse on the perpetrator:

The one with whom you find those gods of yours, let him not live. Here before our kinsmen [search my possessions and] take whatever you find that belongs to you.

—GENESIS 31:32, AMP

Do you notice that curse of death in Jacob's words? It is my personal belief that Jacob spoke prophetically concerning the sin of Rachel's idolatry. A death structure is erected when one bows down to a false idol. Rachel's sin, to bring false idols into Jacob's camp, later opened the door to death when she gave birth to her second son. Upon the birth of Benjamin, Rachel died.

Still, out of His mercy, even knowing Rachel would later possibly bow down to the false gods of her childhood, God was committed to blessing her. Scripture recalls these powerful and priceless words concerning Rachel: "Then God *remembered* Rachel." He had answered her years of pleading, and He *remembered* her. His thoughts were pregnant with a life-giving force for her to produce life.

JACOB'S PERSONAL BATTLES

Through his wives and maids, Jacob was blessed with many offspring. Yet he, too, experienced a "despised" season in which he strongly felt the accusations of his Accuser. For years Jacob suffered under the deception and manipulation of his father-in-law, Laban. I am sure that all the time Laban was tricking him and deceiving him and stealing from him, Jacob faced many accusations of the evil one. I am sure that his battle with his Accuser raged for years.

Furthermore, Jacob may have been tempted to condemn himself with words fueled by the Accuser. The Accuser probably told Jacob lies such as:

- "You should have been more alert and mentally astute than to marry and lie with the wrong woman."

- "How could you lie with a woman you do not love?"

- "You have destroyed your life and messed up your entire destiny."

- "You are stuck with a woman whom you do not love."

- "How can God ever bless you for what you have done?"

- "You stole the birthright from Esau. Now God can take from you."

- "You deserve everything Laban has done to you."

Yes, the Accuser probably battled Jacob with many harassing thoughts, but Jacob chose not to focus on them. Instead he pressed further into a season of completion. Jacob's determination baffles me at times. Just like Job, Jacob just trusted God and moved forward. And because of his faithfulness to the Lord, God *remembered* him and blessed him mightily.

Now let's look at some other biblical examples of God's *remembering*.

GOD REMEMBERED NOAH

Scripture describes the end of Noah's flood experience: "And God [earnestly] *remembered* Noah and every living thing and all the animals that were with him in the ark" (Genesis 8:1, AMP, emphasis mine).

After being in the ark for forty days and forty nights, God *remembered* Noah. Noah had been through his own deep waters (pun intended). He built an ark, probably battled the Accuser as the enemy attempted to persuade him to stop the building process. Then he was locked up for months and months with animals and his family—quite a challenge, as we can imagine. Finally, the Lord rolled the waters back so the land would dry and Noah and his family could disembark. As a sign that God would never again destroy mankind by flooding the earth, God placed a rainbow in the heavens as a sign for us to *remember* His covenant—and as a sign that *He* remembered His covenant.

GOD REMEMBERED JOSEPH

God remembered Joseph, too. Actually, God "marked" Joseph long before his brothers accused and betrayed him (the Accuser at work), tossed him into a pit and sold him as a slave. We all know Joseph's story, and it is a wonderful testimony to God's remembrance.

First of all, Joseph was the son of Rachel and Jacob. He was the baby conceived when God *remembered* Rachel. So from the moment of his conception, he was marked by God. His very name even speaks to his destiny. *Joseph* means "God will add, increase, multiply and bless." When Rachel named Joseph, she was first speaking a prophetic word into her own future—that God would bless her with another child. But the name was also a prophetic word over Joseph's life, a promise of his destiny, that God would add to him, increase him, multiply him and bless him.

Second, do you recall the beautiful coat that Joseph's father, Jacob, gave him? Today we often refer to it as "Joseph's coat of many colors." The garment was a sign of favor and Joseph's being "marked" by God. When God marks His people in this way, long before His season of remembrance, it is as if He is "dog-earing" a page in our history so that He can refer back to it later when the time is right. He marks us as a sign and a promise that He will remember; He will not forget.

Later in Egypt, Potiphar's seductive wife falsely accused Joseph— a clear incidence of the Accuser at work again. Joseph was thrown into prison, and while he was there he interpreted the butler's dream. After giving the interpretation, Joseph said, "Remember me and . . . mention me to Pharaoh" (Genesis 40:14). The word for *remember* here means much more than simply "to recall," because it involves pregnancy and an action expected.

Just as God took action when He *remembered* Rachel, God took action with Joseph, too. Joseph waited for years to be remembered by God. Finally, in His season, God caused the butler to take action and *remember* Joseph. Let's observe Joseph's breakthrough:

> Until the time that his word came: the word of the LORD tried him. The king sent and loosed him; even the ruler of the people, and let him go free. He made him lord of his house, and ruler of all his substance: To bind his princes at his pleasure; and teach his senators wisdom. Israel also came into Egypt; and Jacob sojourned in the land of Ham. And he increased his people greatly; and made them stronger than their enemies.
>
> —PSALM 105:19–24, KJV

Joseph's release from prison to a place of prominence came because when the word of the Lord "tried" him, Joseph held fast to his hopes that God would *remember* him and later bless him. After all, he was marked with favor and marked to be remembered. God remembered Joseph by using another man to open the door to Joseph's freedom and season of great favor.

It is easy to become encouraged as we study the life of Joseph. His birth was a testimony of God's remembrance, and his life was a testimony of God's remembrance, too.

And, believers, it is the same for us today. If we are in the pit of despair, we must not allow the Accuser to tempt us to remember our past, our pain or our trauma. Believe me, when we are suffering we are prime targets for his lies. But we must *remember* both Joseph and Job and how they chose to focus on God's goodness while in the pit of despair. Like us, neither of them knew what was really inside of their hearts until they were tested. And God allowed the Accuser to test them because He had already planned to bless them with double portions after the testing. He did that for Job, and then He did the same for Joseph.

The word *remember* is a pregnant word. Though we may not have recognized it before, it is a word full of potential. We need to choose to *remember* events with faith and not despair. We must choose our thoughts. God says to remember not the former things, which means we should not allow the Accuser to remind us of pain and trauma. Painful memories keep us stuck. But if we realize God's faithfulness during the trauma and focus on His mercy and are thankful, then we can cycle out of pain.

Believer, if you feel you are in the pit and the Accuser is knocking at your door, do not answer it. If he is ringing on the doorbell of your heart threatening to enter, drown him out with a song of praise to God. Doing so will override the chimes of his deceit.

GOD REMEMBERED ME

As I am writing this chapter, I have been enduring my own tests—in more ways than one. Allow me to explain because I am pregnant with a mighty testimony. Indeed, God has *remembered* me.

I spent last year laboring to train the first-year students at our Zion Ministries' Prophetic Ministry Training School in Bedford, Texas. The entire year I had deliberately planned my travel schedule to be home and minister at our First Friday Fire mini-conferences and training sessions once a month. At times it was quite difficult to travel and minister in different places, while continuing to write, and then be "on" again every first Friday of each month. Many of you understand the stress of multiple responsibilities such as I faced last year.

In December 2009, I was to speak at the training school to the first-year students who had just been graduated. On the day I was to speak, I lay down to rest before the service. I was watching television, a show about horse training, when suddenly—and I do mean *suddenly*—my mind went blank. I could remember absolutely nothing in the past. Now you must understand that my horses are my pets. I love them. But none of my thoughts were connecting, and I could not remember my beloved horses' names. I could not even put sentences together. I ran downstairs to talk to my husband, and he walked me through some things to see if I *remembered* them. I could focus on who I was, my address and phone number, but there were huge gaps in my memory bank. And I still could not connect certain thoughts and events that were important to me. I was confused, disoriented and scared, to say the least.

We decided that Mickey would have to minister that night and that he should drop me off at the hospital. I had to force him to go on and preach because he was so worried about me. He called our daughter and my sister, who later met me at the hospital to support me. He also made a phone call to our faithful intercessors, who were already at the First Friday service, to have them begin to cover me in prayer.

The physicians ran every test during my (spiritual) test—CT scans, an MRI, blood work—you name it. After a few hours in the emergency room, bits and pieces of memory began to return. During these natural tests, however, my faith was seriously tested. Within a few hours came the first diagnosis: The doctors said I had suffered a type of mini-stroke. *Okay,* I thought, *I will have everyone pray that there is no permanent damage to my brain. After all, an author needs to be able to connect sentences.*

I contacted several people for prayer, including my bishop, but a battle in my mind raged. Fear of never being able to write again— or preach again, or prophesy again, or even talk again—grabbed my heart and plagued my thoughts. Then, when I was assigned to a more permanent type of room in the hospital, I panicked. *So I am going to be here a while? Where is my computer? What if I get a download from heaven and need to write? And if I receive one, can I even write it?*

It was a horrible night. My potassium was low, and I had to have IV drips. The nurses could not find a vein that did not roll on them, so I was a pincushion for a few hours. All of this involved several more calls to the intercessors. I was instructed to take deep breaths while they poked my skin with a needle that seemed the size of a large fence post, but nothing eased the pain. I have been told that I have a high tolerance for pain, but still I moaned, groaned, tossed and turned all through the night. By morning, I was completely undone.

More tests were scheduled for the next day. It was now a Saturday. It was 39 degrees outside and the chill leaked through the hospital windows. I was cold, covered in blankets and still shivering. When the attendant arrived with the wheelchair to take me for testing, my precious nurse entered the room and said, "Sandie, take every blanket you can with you; it is really cold where they are taking you." Without hesitation, I grabbed about ten pounds of blankets and perched in the wheelchair. I positioned the blankets over and around me and then realized my bare feet were dangling. I had misplaced my hospital socks, and my feet were icy cold. "Where are the little metal footrests for my feet? I want to cover them with the blanket."

Quite pointedly, yet with a tone of apology, the attendant said, "The footrests are broken. You will just have to dangle your feet. But be careful that you do not get a toe caught under one of the wheels."

Great. As if I did not have enough to be concerned about. I froze all the way to the testing room. By the time I went from my room on the fourth floor, waited getting onto and off of the elevator, and got down to the first floor to the testing room, my feet were almost blue. As the orderly pushed me quickly down the hall I realized my face was freezing. *I should have asked for a ski mask,* I thought. It seemed that he was pushing me at Mach 3 speed down the hallways, and the cold wind was hitting my face so hard I thought I might be marked with windburn and chapped lips. "Hey, can you slow down a little?" I laughed, but I was also serious.

"Oh, I am so sorry. I get complaints about that all the time. I get focused on my next project. You know, like dropping you off and taking another patient back to his room. We are so busy, and the waiting line is long."

"What do you mean . . . waiting line?" I cocked my head to look at him, eyebrows lifted, exposing my angry look. By now I was somewhat coherent and could carry on a conversation.

"The 'line to get the test done' *and* then the 'return to the room' line." He went on to say, "Do you *remember* how long you waited in the emergency room before you got to a permanent room?"

"Yes," I told him, "it seemed like forever."

"Well, there was a line of ten to twenty people waiting for rooms last night. It is kind of like that today for people waiting for tests and returns to the room."

At that moment I was overwhelmed. Tired, sleepless, concerned and cold. I could easily have given up, but I had a choice. I chose not to let my mind remember my previous fifteen hours of torment, so I began to pray. I tried to remember certain biblical passages, but could not fit them together, thanks to my "brain freeze" (pun intended). I therefore switched channels in my brain to remember how God had brought me through so much over my lifetime. I remembered how He had delivered me from anorexia nervosa and bulimia thirty years earlier; how He had healed my body from a deadly blood disorder; how He prophetically had kept me safe, sane and stable. Through the long waiting line and through all the difficult tests, I focused on these things. Yet it was truly a battle of and for the mind, and the Accuser knew it.

The Accuser attempted to accuse God falsely in every possible way. Though my own thoughts would still not connect entirely, it was amazing how clear the enemy's thoughts were. I heard his defiling voice say, "You will never be the same. Even if you come out of this, it will just happen again." Fear rushed over my mind and body almost to panic-attack level. If I could not *remember* God's faithfulness, I tried to sing a song to give Him praise. *A mighty bulwark is our God . . .* was all I could recall, so I sang it aloud—over and over and over. It was like an automatic rewind. Everyone in the waiting line probably became annoyed, but I sang anyway. Now that I remember, the Word tells us to "sing over the barrenness of our womb." I needed the "womb" of my mind, which was truly barren, to *remember* what God had spoken over me. Yet I could not remember, and therefore did not know how to expect a great breakthrough in my situation. But God *remembered.*

You see, I still have a destiny to fulfill. God has promised me an extended life and I still have dreams that He has promised to fulfill.

After the extensive testing, I was informed that what I had experienced did not permanently damage the brain. It was not a stroke, but something rather close to one. It seems as if I experienced what is referred to as Transient Global Amnesia, which can be considered a precursor to a stroke.

God remembered me. He remembered His promises to me. You see, God has promised me an extended life. I still have a destiny to fulfill. I keep reminding God of His promises to me. In fact, I am standing on a promise that He gave me years ago, which comes from Deuteronomy 33:25. It says, "And as your days, so shall your strength be" (RSV).

These words originally were spoken by Jacob over his son Asher. Observe the entirety of this passage:

> Blessed above sons be Asher; let him be the favorite of his brothers, and let him dip his foot in oil. Your bars shall be iron and bronze; and as your days, so shall your strength be.
>
> —Deuteronomy 33:24–25, RSV

This was a powerful prophetic word spoken over Asher, but it also is a prophetic promise to us as God's children. When He says that our "bars shall be iron and bronze," He is promising us clearly that we are strong and protected. Being in Christ Jesus means that we are protected as if by a well-fortified castle or fortress. This is why Jesus promised to be our strength, high tower and fortress. The Amplified Version uses this wording: "Your castles and strongholds shall have bars of iron and bronze; and as your day so shall your strength, your rest and security, be" (Deuteronomy 33:25, AMP).

Beloved, if we are "in Christ Jesus," then we are therefore "kept" by God. What an awesome thought! Though God allows a Job testing, we simply need to trust His safekeeping.

REMEMBER MEANS "SACRIFICE"

The word *remember* also implies a "sacrifice." Just as God remembered us by sacrificing His Son on the cross so that we might live, we too must remember God and present Him with a sacrifice.

What is the sacrifice that is connected to *remembering*? It involves laying down ourselves so that we surrender to His timing for our lives. It means sacrificing our time, energies and *self* as a burnt offering. But even more, it involves our giving Him praise and thanks even during difficult challenges.

When Rachel chose to seek God, rather than her idols, as she waited upon a child (this was before she stole the idols from her father's house), she was choosing to remember God, and He in turn remembered her. Jacob struggled with the accusations of his

Accuser, but he laid down his life as he served his Uncle Laban all those long years and chose to believe the promises God had given him. Because he remembered God, God remembered him and blessed him beyond measure. When Noah was faithful to build the ark to the exact specifications God had given him, even though it took him years and years, he was laying down himself as a sacrifice, and God remembered and saved Noah and his family. When Joseph chose to lay down his life and serve God and others even as a slave and a prisoner, he was sacrificing to and remembering the Lord. And God remembered Joseph and blessed him. And perhaps the best example of all is Job, who chose to follow the Lord no matter what the Accuser threw at him, and as a result God remembered him and blessed him tenfold.

In the same way, we must lay down our lives as living sacrifices to the Lord. We must remember Him and trust Him in faith and believe with thankful hearts that He will remember us. If we, on the other hand, listen to the lies of our Accuser, who tells us, "He is not worthy of your praise. He does not deserve your worship. God does not remember you; why should you remember Him?" then we are placing ourselves—and the lies of the Accuser—above God. May it never be—we must never allow our hearts to become unthankful.

BARRENNESS

We all have faced barrenness in our own lives. Perhaps you have struggled with physical barrenness—an inability to bear children. Perhaps your barrenness is in other areas, such as:

- Barrenness in finances.
- Barrenness in relationships.
- Barrenness in hopes and dreams.

- Barrenness in goals.
- Barrenness in love.

Did that get you thinking? I encourage you right now to grab that pen or pencil and write down your thoughts concerning a barren situation that is hindering your trust in God at this moment in your life.

What has the Accuser said to you concerning your situation? Write it in the space below:

1.

2.

3.

Now find Scriptures that confess the promises of God over your barren situation. For instance, if you have believed that you are destined to remain inferior and inadequate, seek Scriptures that say you are strong and not weak, blessed and not cursed, etc. Write your promises below:

THE BOW

Dear believers, Scripture is full of God's remembrances. He remembered Abraham when He gave a son, Isaac, to Abraham and Sarah. He remembered Esther as she faced Haman, the Amalekite who was the enemy of the Jews. He remembered Daniel in the lions' den, Saul on his horse, Rahab as she protected the spies of Joshua, Samson in his final hour—the list goes on and on.

Dear ones, God will do the same for you. He does remember you. Now is the time for you to realize that God is remembering your barrenness, and He wants to bless you. And the Lord does not simply desire to give you a gift; He wants you to know that *you* are a gift. You are special to Him; He loves you. If you are wondering if God *remembers* you, then let me assure you that He does. He has not forgotten what He promised.

I encourage you not to listen to the lies of your Accuser, who tells you that God does not remember you. Choose right now not to focus any longer on your inadequacies or barrenness, but rather choose to believe that God will *remember* you in due season. His remembrance of His promise to you is full of pregnant expectation.

It remains important to keep your internal focus on agreeing with God and His Word concerning you. By this I mean that you must rely on spiritual reality, focusing on His supernatural ability to move heaven and earth to manifest His glory in your life. The Accuser will always seek to make your problems appear bigger than God's desire to bless you.

It also is important not to allow your heart to become hardened during times of waiting on God. Noah's trial was not over when the ark was completed; he had to get inside the ark and endure the Flood. Sometimes we have to gain patience along the way and wait for God to turn our situations around. He always promises to work things together for our good. And the rainbow was the icing on the cake—or the bow on the package—of that promise. The bow was the remembered covenant promise.

God is placing a bow on your promised package. It is a rainbow-type bow—a covenant promise that He will do as He has promised for you. What a gift from God—endurance, developed faith and a trust in God.

Remembering God's faithfulness will empower you to move forward and fulfill your divine destiny. And remembering that God always promises to remember you and His promises to you will seal your faith and connect you securely to your covenant with Him.

Dear one, rise up and declare God's goodness and faithfulness. Declare that God has *remembered* you. Confess the Word and the Scriptures that the Holy Spirit has quickened in you. It is your breakthrough time.

- **B**elieve.

- **R**ejoice.

- **E**njoy His presence.

- **A**sk, and you shall receive.

- **K**now that He is your God, and nothing is impossible with Him.

- **T**hank God in every situation.

- **H**e is able to deliver you from the snares of the Accuser.

- **R**ead His promises and remain encouraged.

- **O**ffer God the sacrifice of praise.

- **U**se the Word as your weapon against the lies of the Accuser.

- **G**ive God praise—every day.

- **H**ave you remembered His faithfulness? Stop a minute and thank Him for His everlasting love.

9

Lie #8:
YOU ARE NOT LOVED

And when the Lord saw that Leah was despised, He made her able to bear children . . . and she said, "(Maybe) now my husband will love me."

GENESIS 29:31–32, AMP

In the last chapter I told you we would eventually circle back around to Leah, and here we are. I believe Leah's story is worthy of study as well.

One might believe that Leah was fulfilled because she was empowered by God to bless her husband with so many heirs. A closer examination of Leah's life, however, indicates that she struggled with the Accuser.

Leah married Jacob knowing that he was tricked into marriage with her. Leah's father, Laban, switched Jacob's betrothed wife, Rachel, with her sister, Leah, and Jacob ended up marrying a seemingly unattractive woman whom he did not love. He needed, however, for her to bear his children. No honest woman would say that she was totally fulfilled simply by giving her husband children. Sooner or later, the children grow up, and if there is no love between husband and wife, the marriage rarely lasts.

Leah believed the only way to keep her husband's attraction was to remain pregnant. If she could not remain pregnant, then she had to face her fear of losing him. Year after year (or should I say nine months after nine months) she had to become pregnant in order to remain confident in herself. Her self-worth, self-esteem and self-confidence all were connected to being pregnant. How sad.

During the times in which Leah realized she could not bear a child, perhaps while she was nursing, she gave her maidservant, Zilpah, to her husband. And, incidentally, Rachel did the same thing. Envious of Leah's successful pregnancies, Rachel gave her maid, Bilhah, to Jacob, and he bore two sons by her. I could never imagine using this tactic. But then again, how many times do we not trust God and revert to an alternative plan? When we devise our own plan, it is almost like breaking covenant with God.

Leah's entire self-worth, then, was based upon her ability to *remain* pregnant. Here we can relate to three challenges:

- getting pregnant with God's presence,

- *remembering* His promise until we witness the break-through (birthing), and

- remaining *thankful* (which is like being continually pregnant) every day for the rest of our lives.

The Bible gives us one more clue about Leah's struggle with her Accuser. Genesis 29:31 says that "when the Lord saw that Leah was despised, He made her able to bear children; but Rachel was barren"(AMP). You see, God blessed Leah with children because she was "despised." In other words, God felt her pain and, knowing she was despised by Jacob rather than truly loved, He decided to bless her with children. The word *despised* seems like a strong word and a rather cruel translation. The King James Version uses the word *hated*, which is not much better than *despised*. So let's study this translation from a different angle.

Strong's tells us that the Hebrew word used in this passage is *sane* (pronounced saw-nay), which means "hatred" but also is closely linked with the word *enemy*.[1] Could it possibly be that Leah had an enemy, the Accuser, who hated her?

I do not believe that Jacob *hated* Leah. I believe he loathed the fact that he had been cheated out of marrying his first love. Leah picked up on it and was never able to lock in to her self-worth. She believed she was unloved because that is what the enemy told her, and she bought in to his lies. As she listened to the lies of her Accuser, all of her worth was wrapped around being able to conceive and give birth. Most women feel ashamed when the pregnancy matures and they feel they "look like they have swallowed a watermelon." Leah, on the other hand, felt wonderful only when she was nine months pregnant.

As she bought in to the lies of her Accuser, threatening her with whispers of rejection and self-loathing, can you imagine her being at the point of insanity fretting over whether or not her husband could even bear to sleep with her? Can you imagine the rejection she must have felt? Shame fueled her need to become pregnant.

Genesis 29:32 says this about Leah's firstborn:

> And Leah became pregnant and bore a son, and named him Reuben [See, a son!]; for she said, Because the Lord has seen my humiliation and affliction; now my husband will love me. (AMP)

It is clear, therefore, that Leah dealt with her humiliation and affliction with a desire to be recognized through pregnancy. Because she did not believe she was loved, she sought to have more and more children who would love her.

MORE SONS

Leah had two more sons, Levi and Simeon. But it was not until she birthed Judah that she perhaps began to understand her true worth, for it was then that she truly was able to praise the Lord with her entire being:

> [Leah] became pregnant again and bore a son, and said, Because the Lord heard that I am despised, He has given me this son also; and she named him Simeon [God hears]. And she became pregnant again and bore a son, and said, Now this time will my husband be a companion to me, for I have borne him three sons. Therefore he was named Levi [companion]. Again she conceived and bore a son, and she said, Now will I praise the Lord! So she called his name Judah [praise]; then [for a time] she ceased bearing.
>
> —Genesis 29:33–35, AMP

I believe that when Leah bore Judah, she no longer was driven by the need to bear children. Perhaps she was overcoming the lies of her Accuser and understanding her true value in the Lord. Perhaps she had realized that she was indeed lovable.

As is evidenced by the meaning of Judah's name ("praise"), Leah had learned to praise God, and her striving was over. Though she eventually gave her maid to Jacob who gave him more children, Leah was not intimidated and driven as she had been in the past.

Furthermore, when Leah later named her fifth son Issachar, I believe it was with intention. Prophetically, the tribe of Issachar was the one that understood God's times and seasons. Leah recognized her time of shifting into a new season and prophetically named Issachar to become the head of God's tribe with this gifting. Ultimately, God's will prevailed over Jacob and his two wives. God clearly blessed Jacob, Rachel and Leah because He made their sons the heads of the twelve tribes of Israel. Thank God that He knows what is best—even in the midst of strife, competition and contention.

THE IMPORTANCE OF REMAINING THANKFUL

Leah eventually learned how to be thankful for all God had given her. It seems that this was the key to her overcoming the Accuser's lie that she was not loved.

It is so important that we not bow our knees to the Accuser and the seducing spirits that work with him. These demonic influences can become strongholds that attempt to convince us that God does not love us—especially during difficult seasons. They will tell us that because He does not love us, He is not trustworthy. These spirits seek to block our ability to remain thankful.

God is always faithful and deserves to be thanked for His goodness, regardless of whether we believe it or not. Our feelings about it are irrelevant. We know He loves us and is faithful because He says He is. We cannot—and must not—believe in our own ability to love or to believe; we must count on what God declares about Himself. During difficult times, our emotions can go wild, but our insurance policy is to remain in His presence and remain thankful.

The New King James Version clearly states that we are to "enter into His gates with thanksgiving, and into His courts with praise" (Psalm 100:4, NKJV). It goes on to say that the reason for us to be thankful and to praise Him is simple: "For the LORD is good; His mercy is everlasting, and His truth endures to all generations." Beloved, if for no other reason, we should remain thankful in our hearts because the Lord is good. He loves us more than we can imagine, He is merciful, and His truth endures—even unto us.

I love how Psalm 95:2–7 states that we go into His *presence* with thanksgiving:

> Let us come before His presence with thanksgiving; Let us shout joyfully to Him with psalms. For the Lord is the great God, and the great King above all gods. In His hand are the deep places of the earth; the heights of the hills are His also. The sea is His, for He made it; and His hands formed the dry land. Oh come, let us worship and bow down; Let us kneel before the Lord our Maker. For He is our God, and we are the people of His pasture, and the sheep of His hand.
>
> —PSALM 95:2–7, NKJV

Dearest believer, we can enter into God's divine presence because the blood of Jesus ensures our entrance. But also, we can enter into His presence as long as we obtain and secure a thankful heart. It is easy to remain in that special place as long as we joyfully shout and recognize that He is God of all gods. Realizing this will remove *self* from its prideful position and empower us to kneel and bow down only to Him. And when we can truly worship Him in this way, we cannot deny how much He loves us.

BEING UNTHANKFUL OPENS DOORS TO THE ENEMY

Let me give you just one more reason to remain thankful. Timothy wrote that in the last days "grievous times" shall come:

> But know this, that in the last days grievous times shall come. For men shall be lovers of self, lovers of money, boastful, haughty, railers, disobedient to parents, unthankful,

unholy, without natural affection, implacable, slanderers, without self-control, fierce, no lovers of good, traitors, head-strong, puffed up, lovers of pleasure rather than lovers of God; holding a form of godliness, but having denied the power therefore. From these also turn away.

—2 TIMOTHY 3:1–5, ASV

For us to remain unthankful opens the door to seducing spirits that attempt to lead us astray. Being unthankful is listed right there among such sins as lovers of self, lovers of money, lovers of pleasure, homosexuality, haughtiness, disobedience to parents, unholiness, etc. How easy it is to link this type of evil spirit with the Accuser. Remaining unthankful, then, links us with those whom God considers to be traitors (to Him and His instructions).

Finally, the word *grievous* is the Greek word *chalepos,* which implies losing strength in the end times.[2] As the Accuser attacks, he attempts to wear us down with his false accusations, doesn't he? Indeed, he is seeking to steal our strength. Furthermore, *chalepos* is derived from the Greek word *chalao,* which means "to strike, to lower (as in a void)."[3] Dear ones, have you felt any blows from the Accuser lately? Do you realize that the enemy attempts to make you void of any promise? As he did with Rachel, he desires to make you barren. As he did with Leah, he desires to steer you away from God's love. That is his plan of destruction, plain and simple.

Let's seek, then, to shift our attitudes from self-pity to thankfulness.

Finally, brethren, whatsoever things are true, whatsoever things are honorable, whatsoever things are just, whatsoever things are pure, whatsoever things are lovely, whatsoever things are of good report; if there be any virtue, and if there be any praise, think on these things.

—PHILIPPIANS 4:8, ASV

I want to mention here that I have written two other books that will empower you to fight other seductions of the enemy. These two books are entirely devoted to exposing the seducing spirits that attempt to abort your testimony: *Destiny Thieves* and *Defeating the Threefold Demonic Cord*.[4] Each of these books will speak to you concerning blockades that the enemy has positioned against you.

DO YOU BELIEVE YOU ARE LOVED?

The Accuser is furious at God, and he is even more furious at your determination to defeat him. You have probably felt the evil seductions of your false Accuser, as well as the temptations to blame God for your hardships. Maybe the enemy is lying to you concerning yourself. What is the Accuser saying to you now? Perhaps he is saying:

- "You are not loved."
- "No one, not even God, could love you."
- "You are despised."
- "You are hated."
- "You are unworthy."

Write here some of the other lies the Accuser is whispering to you:

Now let's bind our Accuser together:

> Satan, you are my Accuser, the one who hates me because I am God's creation. But because I am His beautiful creation, I am loved by Him. God's Word says that "neither death nor life, neither angels nor demons, neither the present nor the future, nor any powers, neither height nor depth, nor anything else in all creation, will be able to separate us from the love of God that is in Christ Jesus our Lord" (Romans 8:38–39). This includes you, Satan. You cannot separate me from God's love, because I am covered in the blood of His Son. In Jesus' name, I command you to leave me now.

Now, dear one, pray with me:

> Heavenly Father, thank You that I am Your creation and that You love me with a Father's perfect love. Thank You that You love me so much that You gave everything for me, even the blood of Your own Son on the cross at Calvary. Thank You that there is nothing I could ever do that would change Your love for me. Thank You that I can overcome my Accuser, who tells me You do not love me, because of the power of Your Holy Spirit, which indwells me. Praise You, Father God! In Jesus' name I pray, Amen.

Dear one, you are an overcomer, called and chosen by God to put the false Accuser under your feet. It is time for you to sacrifice yourself and remember the love and faithfulness of God.

OVERCOMING THROUGH THE BLOOD OF JESUS

Now *is come the salvation, and the power, and the Kingdom of our God, and the authority of His Christ: for the Accuser of our brethren is cast down, who accuseth them before our God day and night. And they overcame him because of the* blood of the Lamb, *and because of the word of their testimony; and they loved not their life even unto death.*

REVELATION 12:10–11, ASV (EMPHASIS MINE)

Precious believer, prepare your heart for the most important subject I could ever pen. This chapter will require more focus than all of the previous ones because of the significance of the blood of Christ Jesus. Please, dear readers, do not skip over this final chapter. This is where it all comes together. I feel that I have written this entire book to lead you to the destination included in this chapter. It is your time to understand fully how to overcome your Accuser and to shift into your purpose and destiny.

We have walked carefully through seven previous chapters, in which I—under the leading, Word and direction of the Holy Spirit—have exposed to you the schemes of the Accuser and how to overcome him. We have discussed the importance of our testimony, of guarding our confessions, of walking in faith and of renouncing ungodly beliefs and lies. We have examined our minds and false belief symptoms, and we have repented. We also have realized the necessity of laying down our lives, dying to self and living for Christ. Now it is time to open our hearts and deeply consider the importance of the blood of Jesus.

We have had quite a journey together and discussed gaining victory over our enemy, but I feel that at times we have basically tiptoed around what the true victory is. Believer, there is neither overcoming nor victory without the blood.

The above passage from Revelation lists the blood of the Lamb as the first way to overcome the Accuser. We have saved the best for last. Jesus' blood was shed for you and me for a specific purpose: to give us life and victory. Every time you heed its incredible significance and benefits, the blood of Jesus will empower you to overcome your adversary, the Accuser.

OVERCOMING

Overcoming is a lifelong process, isn't it? But aren't you thankful that at each bend in the road God is still leading and allowing you to touch heaven once more for revelation?

As we begin our discussion in this chapter, it is important for us to understand just what the word *overcoming* means. The word *overcome* is derived from the Greek word *nikao*, which basically means "to subdue." It is further noted to mean to "conquer, prevail and get the victory."[1] The first time we notice the word *subdue* is in Genesis 1:28 when God gave Adam and Eve the mandate of subduing the earth:

> And God blessed them and said to them, "Be fruitful, multiply, and fill the earth, and *subdue* it [using all its vast resources in the service of God and man]; and have dominion over the fish of the sea, the birds of the air, and over every living creature that moves upon the earth."
>
> —GENESIS 1:28, AMP (EMPHASIS MINE)

From the beginning of time, therefore, God anointed mankind to overcome our enemy and take dominion. Yes, we are called to be overcomers. But it is impossible to have victory without Jesus. Jesus said, "In the world ye shall have tribulation: but be of good cheer, I have *overcome* the world" (John 16:33, KJV).

How did Jesus overcome? By the shedding of His own blood. Dear ones, we cannot win the battle against the Accuser without fully understanding the importance of the blood of the Lamb and having *faith* in its wonder-working power.

THE IMPORTANCE OF BLOOD SACRIFICE

I could compose an entire book solely about the power of the blood of Jesus. From Genesis to Revelation, the Bible keeps the subject of *blood* prominently in our view. Clearly, the sacrifice of blood has been necessary to mankind's relationship with God and to our defeat of the Accuser. I want us to look now at some of the most important blood sacrifices detailed in God's Word.

1. The Garden

Scholars debate over when the first actual sacrifice of blood began, but it is my opinion that the first sacrifice of an animal occurred in the

Garden of Eden when Adam and Eve sinned. If you recall, the Lord had to cover man's sin and shame with a skin covering. From where do you suppose the skin covering came? God had to slay an animal and shed its blood in order to cover Adam and Eve's act of disobedience. While God also shed the blood to reestablish mankind's dominion over sin, I believe this first sacrifice foreshadows our sins being covered by the blood of Christ—the final sacrifice that would ever be needed. It is clear, then, that dominion is due to the power of the blood.

So God Himself made the first animal sacrifice to cover the sins of man. Isn't it interesting that the final and ultimate shedding of blood to cover our sin was made by God also?

2. Abel's Sacrifice

The next biblical sacrifice is described in Genesis 4:4, where Abel sacrificed "the firstlings of his flock." In this passage we see the connection of sacrifice—blood being shed—to the first action of worship. In his awesome book, *The Power of the Blood of Christ*, author Andrew Murray writes:

> We learn from Hebrews 11:4 that it was "by faith" that Abel offered an acceptable sacrifice, and Abel's name stands first in the record of those whom the Bible calls "believers." He had this witness given to him, "that he was righteous." His faith and God's good pleasure in him are closely connected with the sacrificial blood.[2]

The testimony of Abel—his faith, his righteousness and how God was well pleased with him—gives us an idea of how greatly significant the "acceptable sacrifice" is. It is clear that there can be no approach to God, no fellowship with Him, no enjoyment of His favor and pleasure, without the shedding of blood.

3. Noah's Sacrifice

Indeed the Old Testament patriarchs understood the importance of the blood sacrifice. After God destroyed the world with the Flood, Noah offered a burnt sacrifice to God. In order to redeem mankind, God had to have a new beginning, and that new beginning started with the shedding of blood.

It is the same with us today. Our new beginnings begin with the shedding of blood. We would be hopeless without new beginnings. When we mess up, we can start over. All we need is to have faith in the redemptive power of the blood of Jesus and to receive His divine forgiveness for our sin. That alone will defeat the Accuser.

4. Abraham's Call to Sacrifice

After the Flood and mankind's new start, sin prevailed again. But through the divine call of Abraham and the miraculous birth of Isaac, God anointed a people to serve Him. Most of us recall the covenant God made with Abraham. In fact, we call it the *Abrahamic covenant.* This covenant did not occur apart from the shedding of blood. In fact, no covenant God has ever made has been without blood.

Abraham's life was laced with testing. Leaving all he knew and following God required great faith and trust. But his greatest test is well-known to all of us. It is difficult for me to imagine the gut-wrenching emotions Abraham must have experienced when he was commanded by God to offer his own son as a sacrifice (see Genesis 22:1–8). Scripture does not reveal Abraham's emotional condition, but if we stop and put ourselves in his shoes we can better understand the difficulty of his mandate. Of course, God Himself provided the sacrifice at Mount Moriah, and Isaac's life was spared. Yet blood still had to be shed to establish the covenant between God and the generations of Abraham.

Abraham's account offers perhaps the greatest biblical lesson in substitution prior to the death of Christ on the cross. Indeed, as God substituted a ram for Abraham's son that day, He also substituted His own Son in our place. Yes, Christ died for our sins and covered them with the shedding of His innocent blood. Oh, the wonderful blood of Jesus—can we ever stop thanking Him for it?

5. The Sacrifice of the Israelites in Egypt

Later, as Israel was released from the bondage of Egypt, God told the Israelites to sprinkle the blood of the Paschal lamb on the door frames of their homes. Passover then occurred, sparing the lives of God's people and making God's words an enduring ordinance: "When I see the blood, I will pass over you" (Exodus 12:13). By this act Israel again recognized the importance of substitution: The sacrificial blood covered their sins and released them from bondage. Dear ones, when believers sin, the Father sees only the blood that Jesus shed for us. He then passes over us and removes the curse of death from our lives.

6. Sacrifices in the Wilderness

God gave His Law to Moses on Mount Sinai, and Moses then gave it to God's people, the Israelites. Part of that law included specific instructions regarding the blood sacrifice. In the tabernacle of the wilderness that God directed the Israelites to construct, sacrificial blood had to be sprinkled first on the altar, then on the book of the covenant, which represented God's part of His covenant with mankind, and then on the people. As the blood was sprinkled on the people, it was declared, "Behold the blood of the covenant" (Exodus 24:8, KJV). It was in the shedding of blood that God's covenant with His people had foundation and power. Only through the blood can God have fellowship with man.

Covenant power to overcome and be in fellowship with God was therefore foreshadowed in Eden, on Mount Ararat with Noah, on Mount Moriah with Abraham and on Mount Sinai with Moses when God gave His Law.

Andrew Murray points out this important fact:

> There is, however, a significant difference between the manner of applying the blood. . . . On Moriah the life was redeemed by the shedding of the blood. In Egypt it was sprinkled on the door posts of the houses; but at Sinai it was sprinkled on the persons themselves. The contact was closer, the application more powerful. . . . Immediately after the establishment of the covenant, the command was given: "Let them make me a sanctuary; that I may dwell among them" (Exodus 25:8, KJV). [The Israelites] were to enjoy the full blessedness of having the God of the covenant abiding among them. Through His grace, they could find Him and serve Him in His house.[3]

I love the fact that God wants to dwell in me. But unless there is an application of blood over my life, I am an unfit house. Believe me when I say that I am so thankful for the redemptive power of His blood. I have needed a whole lot of redeeming—and knowing my personality and weaknesses, I am sure that I will continue to need that redemption. I am an ongoing project for the Holy Spirit.

Think about your own life for a minute. You desire intimate fellowship with God, yet there really can be no fellowship with Him at all without the shed blood of Jesus. Neither can we defeat the Accuser without Jesus' blood. Aren't you thankful that Christ went to the cross?

WHAT JESUS AND THE APOSTLES TAUGHT ABOUT THE BLOOD

The biblical importance of blood sacrifice is not a fact outlined solely in the Old Testament. The New Testament is full of accounts and references that reiterate the significance of it, and arguably it is even more important under the New Covenant.

1. John the Baptist

When John the Baptist spoke of Christ's coming, he described Jesus as having a dual office. John called Jesus "the Lamb of God, which taketh away the sin of the world" (John 1:29, KJV) and also as "he which baptizeth with the Holy Ghost" (verse 33).

2. Jesus Himself

The Lord Jesus declared that His death on the cross was the purpose for which He came to the earth and that the shedding of His blood was necessary. He was the ransom for many (see Matthew 20:28), and by the shedding of His blood He obtained for us a new life. Beloved, can you comprehend that your new life of victory and overcoming your adversary is because of the shedding of Christ's blood? I am sure that your heart is being made more tender as you understand that at the cross Jesus was thinking of you.

3. After Jesus' Death on the Cross and His Resurrection

After the resurrection, the apostles no longer knew Christ after the flesh (see 2 Corinthians 5:16). The epistle to the Hebrews teaches that the Old Testament temple service was now unprofitable and that God desired to live in the hearts of man. All of the practices of the Old Testament had passed away, and deep spiritual truths concerning the will of heaven were unveiled. The revelation of Christ, His blood and God's perfect will unfolded through the teaching of the Holy Spirit.

ETERNAL TRUTHS REGARDING THE BLOOD

Some vital New Testament Scriptures detail the significance of Christ's blood. Hebrews tells us that "by his own blood he entered in once into the holy place, having obtained eternal redemption for us" (Hebrews 9:12, KJV). And I love this Scripture concerning the blood: "The blood of Christ . . . [will] purge your conscience" (Hebrews 9:14, KJV). Dear ones, not only will the blood purge us from sin, but it also will purge our consciences. How then could the Accuser ever have a place in our thoughts? If our consciences are cleansed by the power of the blood of Jesus, then the enemy has no opportunity to speak lies to us, does he? The blood of Jesus is the central power of our entire redemption.

When we realize these eternal truths, we are freed from the ungodly belief that we are responsible for gaining the victory. In fact, the victory is already established. The real warfare is in our believing that Christ has already paid the price for our victory and then standing in faith with the word of our testimony. Sure, we still have to do spiritual warfare, but we fight from the victory and not to the victory—because Christ has already won the battle for us.

But keep this in mind, too: Even though the price has already been paid through the shedding of His blood, we must daily surrender our lives to Him. Paul said: "[I assure you] by the pride which I have in you in [your fellowship and union with] Christ Jesus our Lord, that I die daily [I face death every day and die to self]" (1 Corinthians 15:31, AMP).

Believers, remember that even though we have immediate victory because of the blood of Jesus, we still overcome through the power of our testimony and dying to ourselves.

Our need for faith and a continual relationship with Him is eternal. Without the foundation of faith in the blood, however, we have no assurance of victory. We are to surrender ourselves wholly to God in prayer and faith and put our trust fully in Him and His ability to overcome the Accuser.

The revelation of the power of the blood is the motor in your faith vehicle. The motor keeps an auto running. Of course, an automobile cannot even start without fuel, but the motor is what "turns" everything. You can have gasoline, but if the motor is broken then you can go nowhere. In the same way, once revelation is hidden in your heart and mind, it can empower the motor. The motor is our faith, which keeps us moving forward in power and authority.

REDEMPTION BY THE BLOOD OF JESUS

Dear readers, the blood of Jesus has redeemed you:

> Knowing that ye were *redeemed*, not with corruptible things, with silver or gold, from your vain manner of life handed down from your fathers; but with *precious blood*, as of a lamb without spot, (even the blood) of Christ.
>
> —1 PETER 1:18–19, ASV (EMPHASIS MINE)

The word *redeemed* means "purchased and bought with a price." Jesus Christ purchased us with His own blood. In essence, He bought us from our Accuser. Though the enemy might find a weakness, target that weakness and later find an entrance, Christ paid the price in advance for our freedom. Satan no longer has a hold on us. If we repent for our weakness and sins, He is faithful and just to forgive us.

In the blood of Jesus, there is power possessed by absolutely *nothing* else. The blood atonement has the power to redeem and accomplish everything necessary for the sinner's salvation. Keep in mind that salvation does not mean simply being "saved" from eternal damnation, but it also encompasses *all* that is needed—especially healing and restoration. In the power of the blood is the miracle-working power of healing, health and wholeness.

The blood of Jesus opened to us the access of heaven. When He died, He took captivity captive, and then He was received into heaven, thus allowing us the same access. We read in Hebrews 9:12

that Christ "by His own blood . . . entered in once into the holy place, having obtained eternal redemption for us" (KJV). Think on this again: *The blood of Jesus opened heaven.* We can therefore say that the blood empowers us to touch heaven with our prayers and petitions.

Scripture also states that Jesus is the Mediator (see Hebrews 12:24, KJV) and that the Holy Spirit gives a prominent place to "the blood of sprinkling" (verse 24). Andrew Murray states that it is the

> constant speaking of the blood that keeps heaven open for sinners and sends streams of blessing down on earth. It is through that blood that Jesus, as the Mediator, carries on His mediating work without ceasing. The throne of grace ever owes its existence to the power of that blood.[4]

What an awesome thought! Believing that the blood of Christ speaks constantly on our behalf frees us from the lies of our Accuser. And according to Scripture, if we have faith and believe, then nothing is withheld from us. If we need healing, then we can plead the blood of Jesus and apply it to our lives and receive it. In fact, no matter what we need, the blood has opened heaven to receive our requests.

WONDER-WORKING POWER

You might still be asking how this power of the blood works. Allow me to quickly explain and make it simple. The power of the blood of Jesus works . . .

1. *through faith.*

It is important to continually search the Scriptures and learn what it teaches about the blood. As you read and gain revelation, your faith will grow. Remember, faith comes by hearing and hearing . . . and hearing.

2. *by gaining knowledge.*

Again, we need to know that we are redeemed not "with corruptible things, as silver and gold" (1 Peter 1:18, KJV), things in which there is no power of life, "but with the precious blood of Christ" (verse 19). Having the correct perception and understanding of the preciousness of His blood empowers us to have a perfected and holy life. The more we understand the redemptive power of His blood and that He has already "bought us" with His blood, then we can more fully experience its value.

3. *by knowing that we need His blood.*

Knowing that we "need" the blood keeps us humbly before His throne. We bring our prayer requests to His throne of grace and receive forgiveness. Knowing also that we need the Holy Spirit and truth empowers us continually to seek His face and become even more dependent on the revelation of the shedding of His blood.

4. *by desiring Him.*

Need and desire are different from each other. Desire is simply *enjoying* Him. It is a hunger and thirst that can be met only by spending time with Him. David wrote in the Psalms: "But his delight and desire are in the law of the Lord, and on His law (the precepts, the instructions, the teachings of God) he habitually meditates (ponders and studies) by day and by night" (Psalm 1:2, AMP).

Desire implies a willingness and great pleasure. Desire is not need-based or problem-based. Desiring to spend time with God brings sheer joy. The blood of Jesus releases blessings to us simply because He loves us and we love Him. In His presence is fullness of joy. Because we have full access to Him, He will release to us His good pleasure when we desire Him. Ephesians

1:9 speaks of God's good pleasure in revealing to us His mysteries and perfect will: "Making known to us the mystery (secret) of His will (of His plan, of His purpose). [And it is this:] In accordance with His good pleasure (His merciful intention) which He had previously purposed and set forth in Him" (AMP).

If we look closely at Philippians 2:13, we notice that He delights in creating power within us, and that power comes by the shed blood of Christ and not from our own strength:

> *[Not in your own strength]* for it is God Who is all the while effectually at work in you [energizing and creating in you the power and desire], both to will and to work for His good pleasure and satisfaction and delight. (AMP, emphasis mine)

5. *through our expectation.*

When we approach God and spend time with Him, we also must have an expectation that the blood accomplishes all it was meant to accomplish. There can be no sense of unworthiness or doubt in His desire to empower us. We must fix our eyes on the wonder-working power of His shed blood and know that we are released from bondage and slavery to sin—indeed, from whatever is hindering us from experiencing the fullness of life.

IT IS YOUR NOW TIME

We started this chapter by looking at Revelation 12:10–11. I would like now to return to this passage. Let's review it again, this time in the New International Version of the Bible:

> *Now* have come the salvation and the power and the kingdom of our God, and the authority of his Christ. For the accuser of our brothers, who accuses them before our God day

and night, has been hurled down. They overcame him by the blood of the Lamb and by the word of their testimony; they did not love their lives so much as to shrink from death.

—REVELATION 12:10–11 (EMPHASIS MINE)

Dear ones, it is time to come into the full "salvation" and the "power" and the "Kingdom" and the "authority" to defeat your Accuser. As you remember and claim the power of Christ's blood, you will overcome. When the Accuser strikes, remember that the blood is your foundation, and you will live continually under God's forgiveness and redemption. It is your "Now" time.

WE STILL MUST REPENT

Beloved, as we come to a final conclusion of this book, let me reemphasize this one thing: The most vital concept to overcoming the Accuser of our souls is the blood of Christ and its redemption. Indeed, Christ's blood was the price for our freedom.

Ephesians 1:7 says:

> In Him we have redemption (deliverance and salvation) through His blood, the remission (forgiveness) of our offenses (shortcomings and trespasses), in accordance with the riches and the generosity of His gracious favor. (AMP)

This means that we already have been forgiven for our shortcomings. Our shortcomings include believing the lies of the Accuser, agreeing with the words of our adversary, doubt, unbelief, unforgiveness, etc. Though we are forgiven, we still must repent. In fact, God desires that we repent. Though we may not fully understand why God expects us to repent since we are *already* forgiven, we still must submit and do so.

I personally love to come before Christ daily to repent and live afresh in Him. To daily name my sins is my opportunity to die to myself. I am not one to bunch all of my sins into a lump sum. I like to name them one by one as the Lord tenders my heart again. It is painful, yes, but a pain that feels so good, particularly once I have finished. Like a deep-tissue massage, it hurts a little—but oh, the relief that comes later.

If I repent, then I am bringing myself to *acknowledge* my sin. The Accuser will always attempt to hinder us from repentance. And he will also surface whenever we draw closer to God.

I choose to continually repent and turn. Will you join me now for some *bent knee* time of intimacy with Him as we finalize our journey? I encourage you now to spend some time asking for forgiveness and thanking God yet again for the redemption that He has given you through the blood of His precious Son.

Please pray with me:

> *Father, according to 1 Corinthians 1:30 and Philippians 4:13, Jesus has been made unto me wisdom, righteousness, sanctification and redemption, and I can do all things through Christ who strengthens me. I am therefore empowered to defeat the Accuser because Jesus has already redeemed me from his lies and false accusations. I am confident that I have the mind of Christ and hold the thoughts, feelings and purposes of His heart (see 1 Corinthians 2:16). I desire to thank You, Lord, for delivering me from this present evil world and causing me to walk in confidence, knowing that I am seated with Christ in heavenly places (see Galatians 1:4 and Ephesians 2:6). I desire today to repent for every time I have come into agreement with the lies of the Accuser. I also repent for listening to the voice of a stranger rather than Your voice. I repent for not understanding the power of the blood of Jesus and therefore not walking in Your power. I am now aware that because of the blood, I have victory over my Accuser. I offer up praise and thanksgiving to You for all You have done for me. I will no longer draw back or shrink in fear because of the Accuser. Rather, I will achieve my destiny. I realize that I was bought for a price and paid for with the blood of Christ. I will therefore arise and boldly declare Your name forevermore. In the name of Jesus I pray, Amen.*

DEVIL, I WON!

Well, dear ones, here we are at the end of our journey. We have covered much territory concerning the silencing of our Accuser, haven't we?

I have always become emotional as I write the final words of the books I have written. I get involved just as much as you do along the way. I have walked with each of you and studied the lies of the Accuser. Together we have examined all eight deceptions attached to the eight lies and recognized our need to repent from believing them.

I once more became overwhelmed with God's love for me as I wrote this last chapter concerning the blood of Jesus, and I am sure that you have become even more enlightened concerning His love for you. This last chapter has reminded us that without the blood of Jesus we are totally powerless against the Accuser. Oh, praise His holy name! Aren't you grateful that Christ has paid the price for your freedom?

I am so proud of you for desiring to be free and for journeying with me. But more importantly, I am certain that God is proud of you.

I want to leave you with a final thought, and that is to always "be strong and take heart, all you who hope in the Lord" (Psalm 31:24). I know that you will desire to remain intimate with God, because it will activate your hope and you will be empowered to silence the Accuser when he rises up to falsely accuse you.

Dear ones, you are victorious over your false Accuser. Now take a deep breath, and then begin to rejoice. As you rejoice, your joy will be full. The joy of the Lord is your strength, so be strong and do mighty exploits in His name.

It is okay to be proud of your victory. Go ahead and give someone a high five. Showing off can be a good thing. It says, "Devil, I won!"

Love and blessings to each of you, precious ones,
Sandie

NOTES

INTRODUCTION

1. James Strong, *Strong's Exhaustive Concordance of the Bible* (Peabody, Mass.: Hendrickson Publishers), 3180.

CHAPTER 1—THE ACCUSER

1. *Strong's*, 8056.
2. Sandie Freed, *Destiny Thieves: Defeat Seducing Spirits and Achieve Your Purpose in God* (Grand Rapids, Mich.: Chosen Books, 2007).
3. Ibid., 148.
4. *Strong's*, 102.

CHAPTER 2—LIE #1: I WILL "COMFORT" YOU

1. Dr. Judson Cornwall and Dr. Stelman Smith, *The Exhaustive Dictionary of Bible Names* (Gainesville, Fla.: Bridge-Logos, 1998), 65.
2. Cornwall and Smith, 41.
3. *Strong's*, 6696.
4. *Biblesoft's New Exhaustive Strong's Numbers and Concordance with Expanded Greek-Hebrew Dictionary* (Biblesoft, Inc., and International Bible Translators, Inc., 1994, 2003).

CHAPTER 3—LIE #2: SHAME ON YOU

1. *Strong's*, 7343.

2. Sandie Freed, *Dream On: Unlocking Your Dreams and Visions* (Bedford, Texas: Zion Ministries).

3. *Strong's*, 6754.

4. *Barnes' Notes*, Electronic Database (Biblesoft, Inc., 1997, 2003).

5. *Strong's*, 1823.

6. Ibid., 2896.

Chapter 4—Lie #3: Listen to My Whispers

1. *Biblesoft's New Exhaustive Strong's.*

2. *Strong's*, 3907.

3. *Strong's*, 3306.

4. W. E. Vine, *Vine's Expository Dictionary of Biblical Words* (Peabody, Mass.: Hendrickson Publishers).

Chapter 5—Lie #4: Let Me Build My Fortress in Your Mind

1. *Strong's*, 3820.

2. Ibid., 5426.

3. Ibid., 3925.

4. Ibid.

5. *Barnes' Notes.*

6. *Strong's*, 567.

7. Robert Fausset, *Fausset's Bible Dictionary online*, public domain.

8. *Strong's*, 567.

9. Ibid., 139.

10. Ibid.

11. Sandie Freed, *Crushing the Spirits of Greed and Poverty* (Grand Rapids, Mich.: Chosen Books, 2010).

12. Cornwall and Smith, *Exhaustive Dictionary of Bible Names,* 105.

13. *Strong's,* 6502.

14. Ibid., 3309.

15. Ibid., 1688.

16. *Adam Clarke's Commentary*, Electronic Database (Biblesoft, Inc., 1996, 2003).

17. *Strong's*, 7291.

18. Ibid., 5825.

19. Ibid.

20. Ibid.

21. Ibid.

22. Ibid., 4719.

23. Daniel Webster, *Webster's American Family Dictionary* (New York: Random House).

24. *Strong's*, 6213.

CHAPTER 6—LIE #5: WEAR MY GARMENTS

1. Ibid., 2280.

2. Ibid., 6437.

3. Ibid., 1497.

4. Ibid., 2502.

5. Ibid.

6. Ibid., 6797.

7. Ibid.

8. Ibid., 6801.

CHAPTER 7—LIE #6: SEAT ME IN YOUR HIGH PLACE

1. Ibid., 3689.

2. Ibid., 998.

3. Sandie Freed, *Conquering the Antichrist Spirit: Discerning and Defeating the Seducer That Binds Believers Today* (Grand Rapids, Mich.: Chosen Books, 2009), 58, 59.

CHAPTER 8—LIE #7: GOD DOES NOT REMEMBER YOU

1. *Strong's*, 2142.

CHAPTER 9—LIE #8: YOU ARE NOT LOVED

1. Ibid., 8130.

2. Ibid., 5467.

3. Ibid.

4. Sandie Freed, *Destiny Thieves: Defeat Seducing Spirits and Achieve Your Purpose in God* (Grand Rapids, Mich.: Chosen Books, 2007) and *Defeating the Threefold Demonic Cord: Exposing Jezebel, Athaliah and Delilah* (Grand Rapids, Mich.: Chosen Books, 2008).

CHAPTER 10—OVERCOMING THROUGH THE BLOOD OF JESUS

1. *Strong's*, 3528.
2. Andrew Murray, *The Power of the Blood of Christ* (New Kensington, Penn.: Whitaker House, 1993), 11–12.
3. Ibid., 14.
4. Ibid., 31.

ABOUT THE AUTHOR

SANDIE FREED and her husband, Mickey, are the founders and directors of Zion Ministries in Hurst, Texas. Together they pastored a local church in Texas for more than fourteen years, and today they apostolically oversee the Zion Kingdom Training Center, which trains and activates the Body of Christ in the fivefold ministries and spiritual giftings.

In addition, Mickey and Sandie have launched Win Ministries in Hurst, Texas, a nonprofit organization to empower women in need. Davis House has been established through Zion Ministries not only to house unwed mothers and women seeking counseling and deliverance, but also to provide spiritual mentoring and impartation.

Sandie is an ordained prophetess with Christian International Ministries and travels extensively teaching prophetic truths to the Body of Christ. She has written seven other books:

- *Conquering the Antichrist Spirit: Discerning and Defeating the Seducer That Binds Believers Today*

- *Breaking the Threefold Demonic Cord: How to Discern and Defeat the Lies of Jezebel, Athaliah and Delilah*

- *Destiny Thieves: Defeat Seducing Spirits and Achieve Your Purpose in God*
- *Strategies from Heaven's Throne: Claiming the Life God Wants for You*
- *Crushing the Spirits of Greed and Poverty: Discerning and Defeating the Ancient Powers of Mammon and Babylon*
- *Dream On: Unlocking Your Dreams and Visions*
- *Heaven's Voice Touching Earth*

Sandie holds a master's degree in biblical theology and a doctorate of divinity. She is often featured on television and radio, where she has shared her testimony of God's healing and delivering power. As a gifted minister in prophecy, interpreting dreams and visions with keen spiritual discernment, Sandie is a sought-after speaker and seminar instructor for her leadership skills, her ability to interpret dreams and visions and her discernment of strongholds over individuals, churches and regions. She is known for powerful, down-to-earth messages that release life transformation and encouragement to church leaders and the Body of Christ.

To contact Sandie regarding speaking engagements, you may reach her at:

Zion Ministries
P.O. Box 54874
Hurst, Texas 76054
817-284-5966
email: zionministries1@sbcglobal.net
website: www.zionministries.us

For more information on Win Ministries or Zion Ministries seminars such as "The School of Prophets," "Advanced Prophetic Training" and "Prophetic Intercession Training," or to see recent teachings, books, tapes or Sandie's itinerary, log onto the Zion Ministries website.